Become a
MEGA-PRODUCER
Real Estate Agent

Profit from a
Licensed Assistant

Robert L. Herd
CRB, CRS, GRI

THOMSON
─────✳─────™
SOUTH-WESTERN

Australia · Canada · Mexico · Singapore · Spain · United Kingdom · United States

THOMSON

SOUTH-WESTERN

Become a Mega-Producer Real Estate Agent:
Profit from a Licensed Assistant
Robert L. Herd

VP/Editorial Director:
Jack W. Calhoun

VP/Editor-in-Chief:
Dave Shaut

**Sr. Acquisitions
Editor:**
Scott Person

Developmental Editor:
Sara Froelicher

Marketing Manager:
Mark Linton

Sr. Production Editor:
Deanna Quinn

**Manufacturing
Coordinator:**
Charlene Taylor

**Production House/
Compositor:**
DPS Associates

Cover Designer:
Rik Moore

Internal Designer:
Rik Moore

Cover Image:
PhotoDisc, Inc.

Printer:
PA Hutchison

Contents

Contents

Contents

Prologue

Anyone who has been in the real estate brokerage or lending business for even a relatively short time will certainly agree that both professions are in a constant state of change—that's a given.

In my 32-year career, I have seen the average completed real estate file go from a few documents with virtually no disclosures or reports to a file that is about an inch thick. Condominium and Planned Unit Development transactions require huge amounts of disclosures that make their files even larger.

The lending business is no different. RESPA (Real Estate Settlement Procedures Act) and other consumer-related disclosure requirements are increasing at a frantic pace to keep up with consumers' ever-growing demand for information. The paperwork alone can be vastly time consuming for even an average real estate agent or loan officer.

The high producers in both fields are becoming totally overwhelmed by the huge amount of paperwork that must be given to the customer in a timely fashion in order to meet the all-important contract issues and the closing deadline. The time spent on these activities can have a terrible effect of the income and lifestyle of a highly productive real estate agent or loan officer.

It is no wonder that the fastest growing phenomenon in both industries is the licensed assistant. These often unsung heroes are rapidly becoming the mainstay and focal point of a profitable and smoothly run real estate brokerage business or lending practice.

Should you hire a licensed assistant? Read on and find out.

Acknowledgements

I want to express my sincere thanks to my wife, Eileen, for her keen insight into what it takes to be an executive-level licensed real estate assistant whose work habits, work ethic, and incredible people skills have made her into one of the top licensed assistants in Southern Arizona.

I would also like to thank Debbie Green and Michael Block—two highly professional real estate agents in Tucson, Arizona—for their contributions to this book by way of their insight into the most productive ways to work successfully with a licensed assistant.

Make a True Assessment of Your Time: What's It Worth?

Your Level of Production Will Determine the Value of Your Time

*R*eal estate professionals and loan processing professionals often tend to discount the value of their time; that is, they don't stop to really assess the value of what they are selling. As real estate and lending professionals, we don't sell property or loans; sellers sell property and banks sell loans. We sell our time and our professional knowledge to people who have a need to acquire, dispose of, or finance real estate.

The more productive you are in either field, the more valuable your time is on an hourly basis, both to you and to your clients. For example, if you earn an average of $30,000 a year as a real estate agent or loan officer and you work an average of 50 hours a week for 50 weeks, the value of your time on an hourly basis is $12. However, if you make that much money working only 40 hours a week, you are making $15 an hour. Where it starts to make a difference is a personal decision, but if your average annual income is $150,000 and you work 50 hours a week for 50 weeks, your hourly rate is $60.

A very important factor in this analysis is that if you have a competent licensed assistant, your business carries on for a full 52 weeks without interruption, even while you are on your vacation.

The current rate of pay for a licensed assistant is somewhere between $11 per hour for a newly licensed assistant with little or no real estate or lending

If you have a competent licensed assistant, your business carries on for a full 52 weeks without interruption, even while you are on your vacation.

experience, to as high as $18 per hour plus bonuses for someone like my wife, Eileen. She has more than 30 years of experience as a licensed agent in two states and has handled over 25 escrows a month for one of the top real estate agents in Southern Arizona. You can sit in on a conversation with her and learn more about how she operates in Chapter 11.

The first analysis that you need to do is to determine how many hours a year you *really* work and where you are on the hourly earning scale. You can then compare your earnings against those earned by the type of licensed assistant that you would like to hire to decide whether it would be profitable for you to hire someone.

Client Acquisition and Development Time

Brain Buffini, President of Providence Systems, says it succinctly when he tells us that we are really in the "client acquisition" business. You have truly evolved into a real, viable business when your role is that of the "rainmaker."

You have truly evolved into a real, viable business when your role is that of the "rainmaker."

Nearly all of us are aware of the huge turnover of real estate agents each year. The main reason for this is the failure to generate enough people to sell property to on a sustained basis. Over the course of my career, I have seen many, many wonderfully talented lenders and agents hit a plateau in their earnings and scratch their heads and say, "Why can't I get past this amount of earnings?"

The answer is always obvious: Each career, whether you are a lender or a real estate agent, has many nonproductive duties associated with it that can eat up huge amounts of what could be highly productive client acquisition and development time.

If you are going to take your career and your earnings to a new level, then you must devote as much time as is humanly possible to the acquisition and development of new and existing clients. Hire

If you are going to take your career and your earnings to a new level, then you must devote as much time as is humanly possible to the acquisition and development of new and existing clients.

someone else to handle the very necessary but nonproductive tasks associated with each transaction.

Writing and Presenting Offers or Taking Loan Applications

Let's look at what starts the "commission check" ball rolling for the real estate agent or lender. It starts when a client says, "Yes, I want that property and I'd like to make an offer on it." If he or she is financing, the lender gets involved as well.

This is where the rubber meets the road in the production of income in our two industries. Everything else is downtime that is necessary in order to meet the client's needs, close the escrow, and get paid. Don't get me wrong—the client's needs are absolutely paramount in the transaction. Many of the remaining things that must be done to get clients happily involved in the ownership of their new properties can very easily be done by someone who bills at less than $60 per hour.

Your job as the rainmaker is to generate business. That means that as a real estate agent you should be spending most of your time in contact with buyers and sellers of real estate, either showing them property or presenting listing proposals to them, not putting flyers in the flyer bin on their "For Sale" sign.

If you are a lender, you need to be seeing customers about their loan needs, and, yes, REALTORS® are customers just like buyers and investors! The last thing that you should be doing is sitting idly at your desk waiting for a credit report to be faxed to you or an appraisal to be delivered.

The Paper Chase: Inspections, Appraisals, Documentation, and More

Over the past three decades the real estate and lending industries have seen a virtual explosion of consumer-related disclosures appear on the scene. It makes you wonder how anyone ever bought a property without them! The fact is, though, that they are with us and they aren't going away anytime soon, so we need to learn to cope with them. The real issue, of course, is to be able to cope with them in a way that doesn't so devour our time that we see our incomes diminish considerably or find ourselves working 70 hours a week in order to meet deadlines in an orderly and proper manner.

Property inspections, such as a home inspection or pest control inspection, are of such a nature that you, as the frontline person on your team, will usually want to be there along with your buyer. This is public relations time as well as an excellent time for you to get first-hand knowledge of the condition of the property in which your client is involved. From time to time, because of what is discovered by inspectors, this will be a good time to pull the plug on an attempt to purchase a property. It is best if you are there for the inspector's recap as soon as the inspection is complete.

Meeting an appraiser at the property can fall into the same category as property inspections if you feel that you are near the limit of the property's value and want to provide the appraiser with additional comparable sales. But if you are comfortable that the property will appraise, then you will probably want to let your assistant meet the appraiser while you spend your time with another customer.

Credit reports, employment verifications, and verifications of bank accounts are best left to an assistant while you, as the frontline person on your lending team, are with new customers. You can always evaluate the package after an assistant has assembled it.

This is essentially known as "time compression." It is really what the effective use of one or more licensed assistants is all about. It gives you, as the rainmaker, the ability to effectively "compress" more clients into any given number of hours without driving yourself crazy or working yourself right out of a good marriage.

This is essentially known as "time compression." It is really what the effective use of one or more licensed assistants is all about.

When Is the Right Time to Hire an Assistant?

The "70-hour" Syndrome

*I*t's 8:15 p.m.; you're still at the office waiting for a counteroffer to be faxed to you by another agent. You are hungry because you didn't have the time to eat lunch as you were showing property and then you met a home inspector at a house that you sold. Your dinner is at home—hopefully still warm, but you won't be eating it for at least another hour. You are so tired, and you have to be at a termite inspection at 7:30 a.m. tomorrow.

This pace has been going on for weeks and weeks. You promised your spouse that you would take a weekend off and take the whole family someplace nice, but people just keep calling you. Your family is disappointed; you've seen "the look" in their eyes, and you are tired—very tired. What are you going to do?

Your family is disappointed; you've seen "the look" in their eyes, and you are tired—very tired; what are you going to do?

Does This Sound All Too Familiar?

You are nearing burnout. You are at a crossroads in your career, and if you want to remain a viable source of income for yourself and your family you are going to have to make some serious decisions very soon.

If you maintain your current mode of doing business, you will surely start to see your nerves fray beyond repair. Your family and social life will begin to come apart at the seams, if it hasn't started to already, and your desire to do your job will fade into oblivion.

Have you already gotten that "look" from the kids when you promised to spend some time with them but had to be with a client instead? Have you seen your spouse struggle to hide his or her look of disappointment when you promised time together and couldn't deliver? Perhaps you're single and you have a date Saturday with a terrific person whom you're really interested in. You are going to spend the day together at the beach, then you get a call from an out-of-state family that you've been working with for three months; they will be in town on Saturday and they are here to buy this time and when can you pick them up?

Any of you who are good at what you do have faced or will soon face the above scenarios. It's a given. I did, too, many years ago when I was a top-performing agent. Top real estate agents and lenders are in high demand; their time is sought out by many, many satisfied customers and clients. It isn't hard to build a good business; it's hard to build a good *balanced* business, unless you do some serious planning.

> *It isn't hard to build a good business; it's hard to build a good balanced business, unless you do some serious planning.*

It's decision time . . .

Stability, Burnout, or Growth?

If what I just described sounds way, way too familiar, you need to take time out to sit down in a quiet place and think through your priorities. Exactly what is really important to you?

There certainly are loan officers and real estate agents out there whose ultimate priority is "the art of the deal"; it's all they live for and everything else in their lives is secondary to becoming number one in their markets. For the most part, they tend to be a rather lonely group and longevity is not one of their strong points. You've all seen them come and go. I recently saw the number one agent of a major real estate company get fired for just such improperly-directed focus. Don't let yourself get to the point of no return with this issue. In both the real estate brokerage business and the lending business you can work as long as you want to, with life just getting easier and easier as you pile up one satisfied client after another—if you do it right. But if you don't maintain a balance with the other areas of your life and carefully place your priorities, your career will almost assuredly end sooner rather than later.

> *If you don't maintain a balance with the other areas of your life and carefully place your priorities, your career will almost assuredly end sooner than later.*

So, What Do You Do?

You really have only three choices, and only two of them are viable. You can pull back to a pace that you can maintain by yourself while keeping the rest of your life intact, you can burn out, or you can systematically grow.

If you simply feel overwhelmed by the thought of hiring additional staff to help you maintain your business at its current level or growing it, then you will need to look at your personal and business finances and decide just how much you can reduce your current level of activity to accommodate your family and the other important matters in your life and still meet your current financial obligations. For many people this is a real eye-opener; between paying for cars, homes and college educations, this can be much harder than it looks, and yes, I've been there too. I was very fortunate to have a highly talented wife who stepped in as a wonderful assistant; we enjoyed working together and she helped to increase my production immensely.

If it is financially viable for you to scale down your operation and you are comfortable with the thought, then that is a very valid position for you. The result will mean less income but a longer, more fulfilling and rewarding career and personal life. Remember, the alternative is burnout.

What About Burnout? How Does It Happen?

Remember the scenario that I posed at the beginning of this chapter? That's exactly how it starts. It's subtle at first, just an occasional tightness or "twinge" in the neck or lower back. Then it progresses into physical pain that gets stronger and stronger with every longer-than-anticipated day. It comes in the form of a weary feeling most of the time; you're feeling negative about things in general and can't put your finger on the reason. People close to you stop inviting you to social engagements and your family begins doing things without you (they're elated if you tag along, but they don't plan on it).

If you maintain your current level of work without getting some good assistance, you will assuredly see these things begin to happen. You are at the threshold of some bad times ahead—*don't let this happen to you!*

If you have taken your business to a level that is causing you to work 70-plus hours a week then you already have in place a strong, viable business platform that will allow you to grow to even higher levels of income, satisfaction, and recognition while maintaining your personal life. The way to do it is by duplicating an important part of yourself through building a support system into your business by hiring one or more capable assistants. This will allow your business to run smoothly and efficiently, even when you are focusing your thoughts and energies elsewhere.

How would it feel to be relaxing at your favorite vacation spot, knowing that you are still taking listings and making sales while you are away?

How would it feel to be relaxing at your favorite vacation spot, knowing that you are still taking listings and making sales while you are away?

Are You Financially Prepared for the Extra Expense?

If you decide to hire a licensed assistant, you will need to have some extra revenue available to pay him or her until you start to reap the rewards of your newfound "rainmaker" time. This can be handled in several ways. Many, if not most of us have the ability to save more money than we do if we look closely at our spending habits. You can probably save some fairly significant money by simply putting a serious budget into effect. If you do, start by budgeting a certain amount of savings each month and take that first out of each commission check. This mindset must be cast in concrete to be effective, but it really works! After you have saved enough to pay your assistant for two or three months you can hire one and not feel any financial stress.

Be sure to consider the possibility of hiring a part-time assistant whom you can grow into a full-time assistant as your business grows. Another alternative is to hire one part-time assistant and if he or she doesn't want full-time employment hire another part-time assistant as the need arises; this opens your horizons considerably.

> *Be sure to consider the possibility of hiring a part-time assistant whom you can grow into a full-time assistant as your business grows.*

Another very workable alternative is to hire a real estate agent as your part-time assistant and part-time buyer's representative. We will talk more on this in Chapter 4.

If you have built an adequate savings account then you already have the necessary funds to maintain an assistant through your business expansion period. Good for you!

Other Financial Resources

- **Borrowing from your retirement accounts.** Be sure to check out the tax implications of this with your tax professional before you withdraw any funds.

- **Bank credit lines.** Yes, you are a viable business and will be well received by your local banker, but be prepared to give him or her a five-year business plan that shows how you plan to repay the loan through your increased earnings.

- **A personal loan from your family.** This can either be quite appropriate or definitely the wrong thing to do, depending on your family or in-laws. Think it through carefully before asking and *definitely* talk it over with your spouse before you ask the in-laws!

Do you have personal property that you can either put up as collateral or sell to obtain the necessary funds? Do you have a little-used boat or recreational vehicle sitting in the driveway? Sell it and put the money to better use building your business; you can easily buy a better one later!

Methods of Compensation for the Licensed Assistant

Generally, three methods of compensating a licensed assistant are used today. The straight salary is a popular method. You simply negotiate a salary upon hiring someone and that is what that person gets, irrespective of how many hours he or she works. My research has found that at this time, salaries average from $1,900 per month for a new and inexperienced assistant to as high as $3,500 per month for a highly experienced assistant.

The hourly rate is also widely used. If your assistant is going to work some weekends and routinely put in extra time for you then you will be well-advised to pay him or her by the hour. Nothing makes a salaried assistant angrier than having to work extra hours and not getting paid for additional time. If you do this routinely to a good assistant, you are most certainly inviting him or her to resign.

As stated earlier, at this time, hourly rates run from $11 per hour for a new assistant to $18 per hour for a highly experienced one. Some agents I have interviewed also pay a bonus of $100 to $500 per million dollars in closed production per month. A bonus incentive is a great way to keep your assistant at the top of his game and always looking for new referrals for you.

A bonus incentive is a great way to keep your assistant at the top of his game and always looking for new referrals for you.

A straight percentage of your earnings is also a very common method of compensating an assistant. If the company that you work for allows it, you simply have the accounting department cut two commission checks each time an escrow or loan closes: 90 percent for you and 10 percent for your assistant. A huge advantage to this is that you can hire your assistant as an independent contractor and avoid the expense of FICA and other deductions and the necessary accounting expenses that come with them. Be very careful to check with your accountant about this issue prior to making any commitment to your assistant.

The Combination Licensed Assistant/Buyer's Representative

Depending on the amount of business that you are currently doing on a sustained basis, you may want to think about hiring someone as a combination licensed assistant and buyer's representative, or "buyer's rep." This works very well for many agents who are just entering the expansion mode of their business.

It is common for an agent experiencing early growing pains to not have enough work for a full-time licensed assistant at first. If you have the chance to hire a good person who wants more work than you currently have available for him as a licensed assistant, consider using him as a part-time buyer's rep as well. This will keep him busy almost full time between the two tasks, and with his help you will be able to service more buyers at the same time.

You need to be very aware of potential time conflicts for a person in this dual role. For instance, suppose you need property brochures in all of your listings this morning to keep the owners happy and you have scheduled your assistant to review all of your escrow folders right after that. You already have a listing appointment. Then you get a call from a lower-end buyer who was referred to you by a good referral source. She's in town for only two days and wants to look at property right away. You, of course, will attend your listing appointment, and your assistant will need to stay flexible and rapidly switch priorities by showing property to this nice lady for you.

Before you refer any of your clients to your new assistant, be very careful to investigate his or her experience level at this sort of thing. If your assistant is experienced, ask for references from past buyers he or she worked with as an agent. Most agents who have assistants in a dual role such as this often reserve the luxury home sales and sales to their past clients for themselves and give new buyers and buyers in the lower price ranges to their assistants.

> *Before you refer any of your clients to your new assistant, be very careful to investigate his or her experience level at this sort of thing.*

You will also need to decide how you will handle the payment of commissions or referral fees if your assistant generates a listing lead for you. Usually the same commission split or referral fee mentioned earlier is appropriate.

Any purchase agreements that your assistant writes should be made in your name and all of the production should go to you if allowed by your company and your Multiple Listing Service. All contracts written by your assistant should state that "this sale is contingent on the review and written approval of *(your name)* within one day after final acceptance of this offer." This is especially true if your assistant is new or newer to the art of drafting purchase contracts.

The most common method of compensation that I am seeing at this time is for the assistant to still get the standard salary or hourly wage for all licensed assistant-related services performed. In addition, he or she receives part of your commission when acting as a buyer's rep, usually 25 percent of the commission that you receive if you give her the buyer lead and 40 percent if she generates the buyer lead.

What Is the Business Climate Like?

Before you hire a licensed assistant, you should take a little time to analyze the current and short-term business climate. We have been in a very long up cycle in the real estate and lending industry. There is no immediate end in sight on a national level; however, your local economy may have something going on that may cause a slower real estate market or less demand for loans.

If that is true then you should very carefully evaluate the continuing level of demand for your services in the near future before you commit to hiring someone.

Before you hire a licensed assistant, you should take a little time to analyze the current and short-term business climate.

On a national level, even a relatively small increase in interest rates usually slows the refinance market down quite considerably and can slow real estate purchases a little. On a local level, if you are in a town or an area that is largely impacted by one major employer, be sure that company isn't sending the jobs overseas and closing the plant anytime soon before you make any decisions.

If you are a REALTOR® then you have the advantage of checking with your local association for local economic forecasts and the National Association of REALTORS® for economic forecasts on a larger scale.

3

The Art of Transitioning

Letting Go Isn't Easy

*T*he fact that you are reading this book tells me that you have been in the real estate or lending business for a time. You have had your share of successes and have built your business to a point where you are very possibly at a crossroads about where to go from here.

You are used to doing it all yourself and doing it entirely your way. A little wisp of a thought may have crossed your mind by now that if you hire someone to take on many of your tasks for you, that person may not do things exactly as you would do them. You are either very concerned or downright scared about letting go.

When I opened my real estate office in northern California in 1974, I felt the same way. I just knew that nobody could do it better than I could. I drove myself absolutely crazy for over two years before I finally got it. It's all in the selection process. Letting go is never easy, but it is the only path to true growth and a well-run business.

> *I drove myself absolutely crazy for over two years before I finally got it. It's all in the selection process.*

The secret to a smooth transition of duties is to first get over yourself, as I had to. Then write down every duty that you must do in order to conduct your business. Separate tasks into "mine" and "my assistant's."

I guarantee that you will still feel uneasy at first, but have regular team meetings and watch your new assistant carefully to see that he or she fully understands and competently performs the duties and tasks that you have assigned. (Try to do this without driving him or her crazy.) Give constructive input when necessary and let him or her grow; it will work out fine.

New Job Descriptions—Yours and the Assistant's

The various job descriptions will, of course, vary somewhat because of how the business operates in different parts of the country. You can edit the following descriptions as necessary. The important thing is to refine them for your area and put them into written form so that each of you is very clear as to your daily duties.

You have essentially stepped out of the real estate or lending business and have entered the lead generation business. You are the rainmaker and your chief responsibility is that of business development or lead generation. As we all know, this is most effectively done through obtaining referrals.

Your primary focus will be to maintain ongoing contact with your sphere of influence, which consists of past clients, a geographic farm area if you have one, and any niche market that you have begun to nurture such as rental homeowners, luxury homeowners, or small apartment house owners. For you lenders it means focusing on a select group of real estate agents, branch managers, and your past clients.

Your appointment book should feature daily activities that get you face to face with people from these three sources. This gives you the opportunity to either get referrals or continue to reinforce to these people that your business is now run primarily by referral. Let them know that you really appreciate their business and their efforts to help you build your business by actively referring people to you.

Second, you will need to take care of some of the client-contact type of escrow issues such as meeting your clients at home inspections or other inspections as you deem necessary. These types of activities should be assigned to your assistant as much as possible except when you want to use such meetings to further your relationship with the client or you think that some type of issue with the property warrants your being there.

Real Estate Agent and Licensed Assistant Duties

Real estate agent duties will include:

1. Conducting listing interviews and taking new listings.

2. Showing property to your buyer clients.

3. Writing and presenting purchase contracts.

4. Presenting offers to your seller clients and counteroffers to your buyers.

5. Negotiating home repair requests. A sharp assistant can share in this duty.

6. Following up on newly referred clients.

7. Returning phone calls from prospective buyers about your listings (sign or ad calls).

Licensed assistant duties will include:

1. Setting up and maintaining files.

2. Scheduling appointments with inspectors, appraisers, and support people.

3. Opening escrows.

4. Maintaining contact with the lender and escrow agent during the escrow and through the after-closing period until all issues are finalized.

5. Keeping the agent advised of missing paperwork.

6. Building and maintaining a list of service providers.

7. Drafting addendums.

8. Negotiating repair requests.

9. Sending copies of inspections and documents to escrow and the cooperating broker.

10. Preparing an informational binder for each listing.

11. Copying an entire file after closing and submitting it to the company.

12. Scheduling time for the client to sign closing papers at escrow and advising the agent.

13. Adding client's name to agent's database after close of escrow.

14. Ordering "listing packages."

15. Filling out listings as much as possible for the agent.

16. Entering new listings into the MLS, or submitting them to the company for input.

17. Answering all office calls for the agent when he or she is away.

18. Checking and restocking property brochure bins as necessary.

19. Installing or remove keyboxes.

20. Greeting clients when they come to the office.

21. Being responsible for all monthly mailings.

22. Handling sign or ad calls and forwarding them to the agent immediately. If the agent is unavailable, showing the property on his or her behalf.

23. Giving general assistance to all clients and customers on the agent's behalf when the agent is unavailable.

24. Assisting all other assistants and buyer's reps on the team as necessary.

25. Handling all faxes and advising the agent as necessary.

Lender and Licensed Assistant Duties

Lender duties will include:

1. Handling the initial meeting with the customer to fill out the loan application. Some lenders will delegate this to an assistant. This is an excellent time to build a lasting relationship that will lead to referrals and repeat business, but some lenders will want to delegate this to an assistant.

2. Reviewing the package after it is assembled by an assistant, to look for any problematic areas such as low FICO scores, poor credit history, high debt-to-income ratios, low appraisals, and so forth. You will then call the client to explain the issues and what you or they must do to correct the problem.

3. Reviewing the package again after all issues have been cleared up and authorizing your assistant to prepare it for submission to underwriting.

4. Contacting the client and others as necessary to comply with any underwriting requirements that your assistant cannot handle.

Licensed assistant duties will include:

1. Conducting the initial meeting with clients to take the loan application, as directed by the loan agent.

2. Preparing and mailing the good-faith settlement statement as required by RESPA regulations.

3. Ordering the credit report.

4. Sending out verifications of employment and sources of down payment.

5. Setting up the file and maintaining it through escrow closing.

6. Notifying the loan agent when all documentation is in and the file is ready for evaluation by him or her.

7. Packaging the file after it is reviewed as required by each lender and preparing it for review by the loan committee.

8. Handling all incoming calls for the loan agent, taking care of them whenever possible and notifying the loan agent of the rest.

9. Processing all paperwork and making all necessary copies required to meet underwriting standards as well as complying with local, state, and federal regulations.

Stay Flexible

Most humans don't readily adapt to change. Having an assistant available to take on much of the work for you is new to you—and it is new to your assistant as well.

Hire well, train well, and have patience. Stay flexible during the "settling in" period and beyond. This whole thing is new to both of you and you will need to make adjustments as you go along. If you find yourself becoming frustrated with your assistant over something, don't let it remain unspoken until the tension is so great that one of you snaps; talk about it openly and immediately. Assess the current situation for shortcomings, gaps in performance and areas of frustration at least weekly at first and talk about solutions. Be sure to have at least a monthly team meeting after you have settled into your roles. This will not only fine-tune your new team operation, it will empower your assistant as he or she will feel that you really do listen and consider him or her a vital part of your team.

Hire well, train well, and have patience. Stay flexible during the "settling in" period and beyond.

Another aspect of meeting frequently and staying flexible is that most assistants are a little further away from the forest than we are and they can see each tree more carefully than we can, if you know what I mean. As they get to know your business and how you operate, you will be amazed at how often they will come up with an idea or a new system or new form that will streamline your operation even further.

If you feel slightly uneasy with the new addition to your team, think how uneasy your assistant feels as well; after all, you are the boss and he or she feels far more vulnerable than you do.

4

Hiring a Licensed Assistant

Licensed or Unlicensed, What's the Difference?

*T*he most visible difference between hiring a licensed assistant versus an unlicensed assistant is the standard of care that you project to the real estate or lending community and to your clients and customers. Remember that we are in a service industry and the higher the skill and education levels that you and your assistant have, the more business you will attract.

We are in a service industry and the higher the skill and education levels that you and your assistant have, the more business you will attract.

Another very important issue is the possibility of your unlicensed assistant's crossing the line and performing real estate activities that require a license. This is a sure invitation to attend an "interesting" meeting at the Department of Real Estate in your state. For example, you are out and your unlicensed assistant is taking your calls. One of your clients calls for you and, during the course of the conversation, asks your assistant what she thinks about a price adjustment. If your assistant gives any opinion whatsoever, she is guilty of practicing real estate without a license. Since she was working for you at the time, you will be drawn into the situation as well. It simply is not worth the risk!

You may also need to explore your state's requirements in regard to advertising. If you are going to advertise yourself and your assistant as a "team" then you will probably be required to register your names with the Department of Real Estate as a team. This rule seems to be prevalent in most states in one form or another, so be sure to check before doing any advertising or marketing using the word "team."

What Characteristics Does a Good Licensed Assistant Have?

People skills are probably one of the most important skills a licensed assistant needs. He or she will interact with your clients and customers on a regular basis and, in essence, is a "substitute you." Your assistant will sometimes work under less-than-desirable circumstances. Assistants need to be good natured all the time as well as thick-skinned on many occasions. (Remember the irate call about the huge number of necessary termite repairs or the less-than-desirable FICO score requiring a "B" paper loan with a higher interest rate?)

> *He or she will interact with your clients and customers on a regular basis and, in essence, is a "substitute you."*

Ask at least two or three questions during the employment interview that will induce a mild amount of stress so that you can get at least an idea about how he or she reacts to it. You might say, "I have several applications for this position. Why do you feel that I should hire you?" Be sure to ask how he or she reacts to unjust criticism; this elicits some really interesting answers. Take it easy with this type of questioning, though, or you could scare off a good applicant.

Good assistants must be very organized. It takes only a glance at the average high-producing real estate or loan agent's desk to see what chaos can and usually does develop. The assistant's job is to put order to it, not once, but forever; can you imagine that in your job description?

He will also need to be a very quick learner. If he isn't already savvy about how a loan is processed or a sale escrow is conducted, he will need to come up to speed very quickly if he is to be of real value to you.

Be very careful to seek someone who doesn't desire to be a full-time real estate or loan agent; otherwise you will become a training ground for new agents and you will end up with assistants walking through a revolving door. That can be very frustrating and even damaging to your business. This isn't easy to accomplish, but if you are very careful during your search and the interview process to ask questions about whether or not applicants are willing to work weekends, how they feel about becoming or continuing to work as full-time agents and why, then you should be able to flush out the candidates who would leave you to become full-time agents in their own right.

Your new assistant will have to be very detail oriented and quickly learn to operate from a checklist as she shepherds your escrows or loans through closing. One of the main reasons that you are hiring an assistant is to free you from the time-consuming details of processing a loan or an escrow so that you can generate new business. If she drops the ball and misses important dates or fails to get documents signed when needed, she isn't much good to you. She must also be able to do this with minimal supervision.

> *Your new assistant will have to be very detail oriented and quickly learn to operate from a checklist as she shepherds your escrows or loans through closing.*

Your assistant should have excellent communication skills. He will be on the phone constantly and the customers, clients, and service people he deals with will view you by the quality of your assistant's ability to communicate both in person and over the telephone.

Where Do You Find a Good Assistant?

By far, your best source of candidates for the assistant's position will be from the real estate or loan agents in your own office, company, or local association. A large number of licensees in any real estate association are doing only a modest amount of business because they don't work well with the pressures of the day-to-day job description of a successful agent, such as constantly working weekends, the uncertainties of a commission income, sporadic evening work, and the other issues that we face all of the time. Many of these people have all the needed skills and would make ideal assistants but they have never thought about it. Or perhaps it has crossed their minds but they have never approached an agent with the suggestions.

> *By far, your best source of candidates for the assistant's position will be from the real estate or loan agents in your own office, company, or local association.*

If you are hiring from within your own office or company, you need to ask the owner or branch manager for permission to contact a candidate before you "raid" his or her staff. You will most likely be better received than you think. Several times a good agent has approached me to ask whether he or she could talk to one of my other agents about being hired as an assistant. I am very picky about whom I hire, and almost all of my new agents end up with great careers, but nobody can be accurate all of the time about whom they hire. If I have otherwise smart, energetic agents who aren't cutting the routine, I am very open to converting them into assistants. I have even suggested it to several agents who have worked for me over the years.

License training schools are another source of good licensed assistants. Contact the owner of the license training school nearest you and ask if you can come and speak to the next graduating class. You will probably find them pretty receptive. As we all know, only a small fraction of the people who go through license training ever become agents or lenders and many of the people who do find that it simply isn't for them. Many of these talented people just don't have enough savings to survive the start-up period, but are otherwise highly qualified. They are prime candidates to hire in salaried positions as licensed assistants. You do run the risk that they will learn the trade, save their money, and become full-time agents, but my experience has been that most of them tend to like the assistant's position. As long as they are paid fairly and treated well, they will stay for a long time.

The business school at your local community college or university can be a very good source of candidates. Call the college or university and find out who the dean of the business school is. Write that person a letter first, telling him or her in as much detail as possible about the position that you are offering. Be sure to mention that it will enhance the candidate's overall business experience while he or she is obtaining a degree. Ask if you can have your letter posted where possible candidates will see it, or if it is possible for you to come and speak about the position to one or more of the classes at a career day.

Most of these students tend to be in their early to mid-twenties. Many of them bring the exuberance of youth with them; however, a great number of them are quite mature and can be an excellent catch.

Don't overlook your own client base. If you are looking for an assistant, you have probably been a lender or real estate agent for awhile now, and have built up a sizeable database of satisfied clients. It is very possible that you have a past client who would make a terrific assistant. These people can vary widely in age and ability. Some of your group will even be retired and looking for a new challenge.

> *Don't overlook your own client base.*

Like newspaper advertising, employment agencies are another option. I have never had to use them as I have always found that so many well-qualified candidates can be obtained from the other sources listed in this chapter. However, employment agencies are certainly a viable option and would probably fulfill your needs if the other options are not available to you. If you run an ad in the newspaper, do not include the salary range; save that for the interview. If you don't care to hire the applicant, don't even bring it up.

Use a Preemployment Agreement

You are about to enter into a "business-marriage." What I mean is that the relationship that you form with your assistant will become a very close one, and you will impact each other's lives in a big way. You want the relationship to be a positive experience for you both. You will expect near flawless work on a continual basis and your assistant will expect long-term employment and a reasonable amount of appreciation for a job well done.

It is amazing to watch owners and branch managers of both real estate and lending companies interview prospective agents. Far too often, they bring candidates into their offices and start to talk, describing their firms, the job, the pay and much more, without giving the candidates the opportunity to ask and answer any questions at all. This is a serious mistake that you do not want to make when you are interviewing people for your new position.

The first thing that you want prospective assistants to do is to fill out a preemployment application. A sample application is in Appendix A. Feel free to modify it in any way that fits your local area and style.

Use of a preemployment application provides a solid basis for you to conduct an interview with someone in a controlled manner, asking all the right questions and eliciting better answers.

When an applicant comes to an interview, have your receptionist give her the application. If a conference room is available, your receptionist can just give her the form and a pen and ask her to fill it out in the conference room prior to your meeting. Another alternative, especially if no conference room is available, is to have your receptionist provide the application on a clipboard and ask the applicant to fill it out while waiting in the reception area prior to her meeting with you.

The Job Interview

The applicant has arrived and your receptionist has just informed you that he is ready to meet with you. Go out and greet him warmly. Your receptionist should be trained to offer some type of refreshments, such as water, coffee, or tea.

Much can be said in favor of conducting an interview at a round table or even using a couple of chairs that face each other, instead of across a desk, which can often be seen as a barrier. However, your demeanor will almost always overcome this issue, once you get used to the interview process. If you have an impressive trophy wall filled with plaques and professional designations, it can enhance your stature in the eyes of someone whom you really like and want to hire. I would suggest that you try both interviewing at a table and across your desk and see which works the best for you.

Ask the applicant if you may take a couple of minutes to scan the application. While you are doing so, feel free to comment on anything that seems to be a particularly strong positive or negative trait or ability and ask him to tell you more about it as you continue to peruse the application. Avoiding eye contact during this initial stage of the interview often gets you better, truer answers to many questions than if you were looking the applicant in the eye.

When you finish scanning the application, start the interview by asking him to tell you a little about himself. Where is he from? What schools has he attended? Is he a college graduate? What college or university did he attend? If it is not on your application, be sure to ask how he heard about your position and why it interested him.

Ask as many open-ended questions as you can, in a paced, controlled manner. Open-ended questions are questions that cannot be answered "yes" or "no," and require an actual response. For example, "Are you a licensed real estate agent?" (a yes or no question) will usually produce a completely different response than "If you don't have a real estate license, you will have to get one for the position that I'm offering. How do you feel about that?"

Using the application as a road map, thoroughly talk your way through the interview, doing much more listening than talking. It is wise to ask at least a couple of questions that will put applicants under a bit of stress, just to see how they handle it. As stated earlier, be very careful not to overdo it or you stand a chance of offending or scaring them and you could lose a good candidate. An example of this would be if a candidate was even a little late in arriving, you could ask, "I noticed that you were a few minutes late today; is this a habit?" If you like this person so far, and his or her response to this is reasonable but a little flustered, just smile and say that you understand completely.

Remember that your assistant will be taking many, many calls for you from clients and business associates and will be a direct reflection on you, so when interviewing potential assistants, listen to their tone of voice, watch their mannerisms, and look for posture, eye contact, and body language that reveal self-confidence, poise, and clarity of communication.

You wouldn't think that someone would come to an employment interview dressed in extremely casual clothes, would you? Well, you are probably in for a surprise! While the overwhelming majority will dress appropriately, occasionally someone will show up in jeans or hip huggers or some other type of totally inappropriate clothing. If you do encounter someone like this—and you will—ask yourself what your immediate reaction will be and act accordingly. You can do anything from telling such candidates that you expected them to be more appropriately dressed and you would like to reschedule, to telling them that they are dressed inappropriately for an interview and saying that you have learned all about them that you need to know and ending it right there, to just going ahead with the interview and bringing up their inappropriate dress during your conversation to get their reaction.

Several years ago I was interviewing candidates for a receptionist position. One young lady who was sent to me by our human resources department wore an extremely short skirt and every fingernail was painted in a different color scheme (one had the American flag on it). The first question she asked was how much the pay was and how much vacation and sick leave would she get the first year. She was an OK young lady who was totally unschooled in how to get a job. I told her that I had absolutely no intention of hiring her, but if she were interested, I would tell her why she was not suitable. She wasn't interested, and that was the shortest interview that I have ever conducted.

Once in awhile someone will be so keen on working for you that she will ask you during the interview whether or not she has the job. Unless she absolutely sparkles and you don't want any chance of losing her, the best advice that I can give you is to say, "We have several more people to talk to, and then we will be contacting everyone to let you know."

> *Once in awhile someone will be so keen on working for you that she will ask you during the interview whether or not she has the job.*

Should you ever hire a relative, including your spouse? It is an interesting and maybe dangerous question. You probably know your spouse very well and can make a reasonable decision. I have seen husband/wife teams many times over the years. Most have been very successful, but I have also seen a few instances where one spouse was absolutely unbearable and surely cost the family dearly in lost business.

Overall, husband/wife teams are one of the fastest growing forms of successful partnership in the real estate and lending fields today.

If your crazy cousin Eloise interjects herself on you because she heard that you were looking for someone and she just happens to be out of work right now (again!), be prepared to handle the turndown in as diplomatic a way as you can, but do not, under any circumstances, hire her. A reasonable way to handle this would be to tell her that you are already considering three or four very experienced people but if none of them work out you'll get back to her.

Never Agree to Hire Someone at the First Interview

Every once in awhile you will interview someone and you will just plain be impressed and you will be inclined to hire her on the spot. It is still better advice to tell that person that you really like what you see and that you will get back to her later that day or tomorrow after you check her references. Give yourself at least a little time to reflect back on the interview carefully to see if, in retrospect, something new and maybe negative jumps out at you. Remember, plenty of people interview very well but can't hold a job for a variety of reasons. You should at least ask for and check references. When you call current or former employers you should always ask, "If I decide that I can't use her, should I send her back to you?"

Nearly all employers are reluctant to give any negative feedback on a current or former employee because they fear civil litigation against them for doing so. But if you ask if you should send the applicant back and you get any form of hesitation or negative response, then think it through very carefully before you hire that person.

During the course of your interview process, you may find that two or more applicants really appeal to you. If this happens, send polite turndown notices to the ones that you didn't want to hire (be nice—they have feelings too, regardless of how many colors their fingernails are). Call and tell the other applicants that you have narrowed the field to two or three (or whatever the actual number is) candidates and invite them back for a second interview.

Picking the right person is going to create a little magic in your life and make it much easier and more productive and rewarding, so be sure to carefully weigh the important factors such as phone voice, bearing and personality, and ability to adapt quickly and easily to new and even stressful situations. Good looks are always nice, but don't make the mistake of being swayed by appearances into a hiring decision you will regret later.

Picking the right person is going to create a little magic in your life and make it much easier.

Lastly, listen to the old "gut feeling." The more you interview, the more you develop a sixth sense about people, and your gut feeling about interviewees just continues to refine itself as time goes on. Listen to it! I really want to reemphasize that point; *really listen to it!* I am now into the fourth decade of my real estate career and I can unabashedly tell you that every time that I hired someone that my gut feeling told me not to, I paid very dearly for it and had to let that person go shortly thereafter. It is very unpleasant!

The Ninety-Day Probationary Period

Hiring employees in the United States these days is fraught with potential litigation for the employer. It is a true epidemic in our society. Since you will be directing the activities of your assistant, he will be an employee by default and you will not be able to hire him as an independent contractor as you may be able to do with a buyer's representative. You may, however, and almost certainly should hire him under an "at will" contract, and for a probationary period of at least ninety days.

During this probationary period you should have consistent weekly meetings. These meetings should be a regular part of your working relationship for as long as you have an assistant because they provide a venue for good, clear communication. During the probationary period weekly meetings are also an excellent way of evaluating your assistant's performance and making any necessary adjustments, providing both positive and negative feedback, or severing your relationship without getting into any legal problems.

As we discussed in Chapter 3, you will each need a clearly written job description. It is important that your new assistant not only knows her duties, but knows what yours are as well. Many times she will field a call from someone looking for you and, knowing your job description and knowing generally what you are doing that day, she will be able to better direct the caller to you or handle him for you.

It is clearly not reasonable to expect maximum performance from an assistant who doesn't have a very clear vision of what you expect him or her to do. The first ninety days is the ultimate best time to set your assistant's

It is clearly not reasonable to expect maximum performance from an assistant who doesn't have a very clear vision of what you expect him or her to do.

work patterns in such a way that they complement your own activities and your style.

During this probationary period it is a good idea to get feedback from your broker, branch manager, or other agents in your office as to how the assistant performs when you are not around. Maria, one of my very best agents, recently hired a young, unlicensed assistant with the understanding that she would become licensed within her probationary period.

People this young often don't work out very well, but her assistant did get licensed right at the last minute. She also got in the habit of showing up about ten to fifteen minutes late on many occasions. When this was reported to Maria, she had a business-level conversation with the young woman and told her that this had been brought to her attention and that it was not proper and wouldn't be tolerated any further. The assistant has been on time ever since. This is a good example of how open, business-level conversation and feedback from others can help you to set the stage for what you expect. Remember, you are the boss, like it or not.

Offering a Person the Job

Your attorney should create your employment agreement, and should be up to date on employment issues or should refer you to someone who is. I have purposely not included an employment agreement here as they can and must be very specific in addressing local, state, and federal issues as well as the specifics of the position that you are offering. Just be sure that your agreement is "at-will," has a probationary period, states that the assistant is to become licensed during the probationary period as a condition of continued employment, and spells out the job description and duties in as detailed a way as possible. Be sure that the job description includes "other such duties as the employer, in his or her sole discretion, shall deem necessary for the assistant to do." This gives you the right to add to or modify job duties at your discretion, as necessary.

A good way to reduce the cost of having an attorney create an employment agreement for you is to talk to one or more real estate agents or loan officers you know who already have one or more licensed assistants and ask him if he has an employment agreement. If he does, ask him if he would mind sharing with you or selling you a copy for a reasonable price. Be sure to ask if he had it drafted by an attorney familiar with employment issues. If you do it this way, you should carefully review it yourself. If you aren't completely comfortable with the agreement, you should have your own attorney edit it for you, adding or deleting as necessary to fully protect your interests. Remember, there is no substitute for good legal services.

One issue that you will encounter when you hire an assistant is where you are going to put her. Space is precious in real estate and mortgage offices and the owners or managers are reluctant to give up productive "agent space" for an assistant who adds very little to the owner's bottom line.

If you have space in your existing private office it won't create a problem except that you may need to make arrangements for an additional desk, telephone, and filing cabinet. If you don't have space available in your office then you will need to talk to your broker or branch manager. Be prepared to have your assistant work off-site if necessary, possibly at your house or at an alternative location. My youngest daughter, Stacy, works for a highly productive agent in Scottsdale, Arizona. The agent has a complete office set up in her home and works from there a considerable amount of time, and Stacy works from there as well.

After you hire your new assistant, take the time to introduce him at your next office meeting and introduce him to your administrative staff as soon as possible. Remember, all of this is probably totally new to him and a little intimidating, so the sooner that he feels comfortable in his surroundings, the sooner he will be able to totally concentrate on the job of making your life easier.

Your administrative staff most certainly has minimum standards of paperwork that must be completed for you to get your commission checks, so be sure to have them set some time aside to show your assistant the ropes. Either you or your broker or branch manager should take him on a complete tour of the office to show him where all of the forms are as well as the fax, copy machines, computers, and forms that are regularly used. If your assistant will be working from your home office or at a location other than the office, you will need to familiarize him with that site as well.

Many, if not most, high-producing agents develop forms that they use internally within their teams or groups. If you have any of these, be sure to completely educate your assistant on where they are, what they are used for, and when and how to use them.

Discussing Financial Concerns

Be sure that you have a salary range in mind before you meet with an applicant to offer him the position. We all want to work for as much money as possible, and if the subject has not been addressed in a prior meeting with the applicant it must be discussed now. If you are not prepared, you could easily pay too much or lose the applicant because you were caught off guard. Have a sheet in front of you that states the salary range for the position and any and all other benefits that go with it, such as payment of Association and/or Multiple Listing Service dues, payment of continuing education fees, initial licensing fees, license renewal fees, health insurance, and so forth.

Be sure that you have a salary range in mind before you meet with an applicant to offer him the position.

If you are including any type of bonus, clearly spell it out on this sheet. Be prepared to explain each of these items in detail. A salary range is probably the best way to present the money issue. If you will be paying your assistant a percentage of your received earnings as Debbie Green does (you will read an interview with her in Chapter 10 of this book), then it is very simple. However, if you will be paying an hourly wage or salary, clearly spell it out and show what rate he or she will start at and explain why. At this time, hourly rates tend to run from $11 an hour to as high as $18 an hour, as stated in Chapter 1.

Appendix B contains a sample interview sheet. Please feel free to use it or modify it at your discretion.

5

Training the Licensed Assistant

The Newly-Licensed Assistant

The Real Estate Professional Assistant (REPA) Designation Is a Must

*W*hether your new assistant is an experienced agent, newer agent, or has never been an agent doesn't matter. To truly support you at a highly professional level, he or she should obtain the REPA designation that is available from the National Association of REALTORS®.

This course costs less than $200 at this time and is given by most license training schools. It is sometimes sponsored by the Women's Council of REAL-TORS® and given through local real estate associations. It is most often given in four three-hour segments, two a week for two weeks.

> *To truly support you at a highly professional level, he or she should obtain the REPA designation that is available from the National Association of REALTORS®.*

The course is very well written and presented and covers every facet of what it takes to assist a high-performing agent in his or her daily activities. I sent my office administrator and my escrow administrator through the course at my own personal expense and it paid off so handsomely that it has become a must-do for every administrative person that I hire.

Company Sales Training

Most mortgage brokerage and real estate companies offer some form of sales training to their new associates. If this is available your new assistant should participate in it. It will allow her to become familiar with the company philosophy and methods of operation and will further refine her skill level, making her more productive for you. She should also be fully trained by your office's administrative staff on use of the forms that are required in order to complete a file.

Your Personal Training

While it is extremely important that your assistant understands how your company and the real estate business work, it is absolutely crucial that he knows intimately how *you* work.

Every successful real estate agent or loan officer has a unique way of conducting business. If you and your assistant are going to work effectively together, he will need to know precisely what you expect from him and when.

You need to create a written document that clearly outlines what you do and exactly how you do it, and what his role is in the process. In Chapter 3 we talked about examples of job descriptions for you and for your assistant; that is a great start, but you will get a lot more value out of those detailed descriptions if you carefully explain what each item on each list means and why it is important.

That way your assistant won't just blindly follow orders without really understanding them. He will be fully empowered to conduct activities on your behalf. This makes a great deal of difference in overall job satisfaction and will further his sense of being an integral part of the team, so he will be inclined to stay with you longer.

Any time that you feel it is appropriate, take him with you when you take a listing, present an offer to a seller, or take a loan application from a borrower. There is nothing like real-world experience to get him to understand what it is that you do, how you do it, why it's so important, and how his role helps you to keep on top of the whole thing.

If he observes you dealing with an ornery buyer, seller, or loan customer, he may be less inclined to want to leave you and do what you do for a living.

If he observes you dealing with an ornery buyer, seller, or loan customer, he may be less inclined to want to leave you and do what you do for a living.

Your Company's Policies and Procedures

Every real estate and lending company has a set of policies and procedures that must be adhered to. These deal with a myriad of different things such as what forms to use and why, when they must be turned in, what constitutes a complete file so that you will get paid, and other clearly operational issues. They also deal with such things as dress code, what the company does and does not pay for, such as postage and supplies, and many other day-to-day issues. Be sure that your new assistant gets a copy of the company's policy and procedures manual and signs a statement that she has read it and understands it thoroughly.

Have your assistant read the manual during the first few days after she starts with you, and then meet with her and ask if there is anything in the manual that she isn't clear about. If she needs further explanation or clarity on anything, review each item with her until she is comfortable with everything.

Communicate Your Work Ethic and the Value of Your Clients

You have worked very, very hard to build your business into what it is today, and you are naturally very protective of it. Your customers and clients have come to expect a certain level of professional service from you.

Can you imagine what they would think if they called you and got a surly, impatient assistant instead of you? Not a pleasant thought, is it? That is why you must be so careful during the interviewing and hiring process and why you must sit down with your new assistant on the very first day and explain in detail not just how you work, but why you work the way that you do.

Sit down with your new assistant on the very first day and explain in detail not just how you work, but why you work the way that you do.

I know a very productive agent who had a top-rated assistant but took her for granted and even started mistreating her. The assistant finally had enough and quit last year. She was immediately hired by another agent who knew of her reputation. The first agent then hired a replacement who many people knew had a terrible reputation for being surly and abusive. The agent was so anxious to find a replacement that she didn't check out the new assistant and had to fire her in less than two months. But while she was on the job, she created more havoc than anyone cares to admit. So be very careful.

Many top agents and loan officers are just plain workhorses; I know because I'm one of them. They love the business and never tire of the day-to-day fun and the challenges that are associated with it. If you are one of these high-energy people, it is wise to bring this up early in your new relationship because if you hire a slow moving, low-energy person, he or she will drive you crazy. Likewise, if you tend to work on a slower, more methodical basis then you may find that a really high-energy assistant will become bored with the pace and will either drive you crazy or quit.

Anyone who has successfully sold real estate or helped to finance it for any length of time knows how very precious the relationship is that you have with your clients. You carefully nurture those relationships just because it's the right thing to do, as well as for the clients' repeat and referral business, which is the lifeblood of both the real estate and lending practices.

The agent who was mentioned earlier lost clients because of the actions of her new assistant; you certainly don't want that to happen to you. You must have a heart-to-heart conversation with your new assistant to stress the importance of your relationships with your clients and how vital those relationships are to you.

Have Regular Meetings for Ongoing Training and Good Communication

Being in synch with your assistant will always be an important factor in the overall health of your business, but during the training period it is critical that you meet as frequently as possible to keep the communication flowing as it should and to see that you are meeting each other's requirements.

Weekly meetings will allow you to discuss any areas that he finds challenging and help him with them; the meeting will also allow you to train him on how to do mailings and other types of

Weekly meetings will allow you to discuss any areas that he finds challenging and help him with them.

client-oriented communications that you need to have done at particular times. You can talk about your respective work schedules and make any changes that are necessary.

It is also an excellent time to discuss each open escrow and each listing that you have and what needs to be done for each one during the next week to keep them all flowing smoothly so that you have happy, well-informed clients.

For you lenders, it is an excellent time to discuss each loan that you have in progress and decide what must be done with each one during the week ahead, as well as talk about any marketing needs that your assistant can help you with.

The benefits of weekly team meetings and the enhanced communication that they nurture are immense. You are very wise to budget a one-hour meeting for this purpose each week.

The Experienced Assistant or Real Estate Agent

The REPA Designation—Should It Be Obtained?

Earlier in this chapter we talked about the benefit of having your new assistant obtain the Real Estate Professional Assistant (REPA) designation to really learn the ins and outs of how to be an effective assistant to a high-producing real estate agent or lender. The question here is, if you hire an experienced agent, does he or she need to go through that course? This is a very personal decision that you will have to make after you have decided that you want to offer a job to a particular person.

Your new assistant may be experienced, but the issue is, how experienced is she and what is she experienced at?

Your new assistant may be experienced, but the issue is, how experienced is she and what is she experienced at?

If she has been a real estate salesperson and decided that she hated working weekends, is she really experienced at putting loan packages together? Does she know how to obtain a tri-merged credit report? Does she have any idea about what a FICO score is, and can she tell a good one from a bad one?

The same goes for the newer real estate agent who is being hired by a busy real estate agent. What exactly is his track record? Just how long did he sell real estate and how successful was he?

Surely many, many fine, experienced agents out there are very savvy about what it takes to be a good assistant, but my experience with sending people through the REPA course has been that it adds so much clarity to the job that even veteran agents who are making a change to the assistant's position get a lot of value from it.

You also need to consider that some experienced people will be offended that you are requiring them to attend what they may consider to be a basic course. You will need to analyze the emotional makeup, ego, and skill level of your new experienced assistant before making any demands about this. If you feel strongly that he would benefit from attending the course, it may be wise to ask his opinion of it first, and then suggest that he and you would both benefit from his attending. Diplomacy certainly rules here, but remember, it is your show.

Familiarization with Your Company's Policies and Procedures

If you are hiring an assistant who is currently, or has previously worked with your company, then she should already be familiar with its policies and procedures. However, it is still a good idea for you to review the manuals and focus on any issues that are potential trouble spots, such as appropriate dress code, long distance calls, and so forth.

If she has not worked with your company before, it is a good idea to require her to attend any company training that addresses the policies and procedures to avoid the development of problematic situations later.

Thoroughly Review the New Job Description with Your Assistant

When you think of hiring an experienced assistant, you can almost make a case that he already knows how to be an assistant. There certainly is truth to that; however, if he hasn't worked for you, he doesn't know how to be *your* assistant and if he hasn't worked for your company he doesn't know the requirements of *your* company. There simply is no such thing as an

If he hasn't worked for you, he doesn't know how to be your assistant.

experienced assistant who knows *intimately* how you and your company work, so every assistant, no matter how experienced, needs training.

Some assistants bring a little bit of ego to the job and you will need to set the record straight, right from the start—there is only one boss, and that is you. Make sure that he fully understands that you respect his talents, but you are the one signing the paychecks and while you are always willing to listen to him about any business-related issue, you reserve the right to make all of the final decisions.

Give him a written job description that spells out in as much detail as possible the various duties that he will be responsible for. On such things as mailings to a farm area or to a sphere of influence, be sure to include a monthly date by which each mailing is to be delivered to the post office. In fact, your mailing program should be spelled out for your assistant an entire year in advance and should include what is to be mailed, such as postcards, sports schedules, just listed or just sold cards, etc., as well as the dates.

Earlier in this book, I outlined a sample job description for you. Using it as a guideline, and with input from your new experienced assistant, refine it to reflect how you work and what you expect from your assistant. Remember, you are a team now and the various duties should be delegated to each of you so as to make the ultimate best use of time for each of you.

> *The various duties should be delegated to each of you so as to make the ultimate best use of time for each of you.*

Be sure to design both of your job descriptions to reflect that the best use of your time is that of the *rainmaker*, or business developer. Your job description should primarily put you face-to-face with prospective and current clients while your assistant's job description should primarily focus on the behind-the-scenes tasks that are required to close escrows and keep clients happy.

Communicate Your Work Ethic and the Value of Your Clients

This should be much easier to convey to an experienced assistant than to a new one because in all likelihood she has already experienced it first hand; however, her experiences may have been much different from yours, and maybe not nearly as effective. That may even be the reason that she has decided to become an assistant instead of continuing to work as an agent.

Everyone has a different standard of care as to how he or she works with clients. Many very good agents just do exactly what is expected, meeting all of the clients' requirements, and that is it; they have no desire to give great service, only adequate. That certainly isn't you; you give world-class service to each and every person you do business with because it is simply what you are all about, and your new assistant needs to know it. This is an immensely important training issue and needs to be stressed right from the start.

You give world-class service to each and every person you do business with because it is simply what you are all about, and your new assistant needs to know it.

You can't assume that even an experienced assistant knows just how precious and valuable each and every client is to someone on a commission income, so take the time to talk this through with her and really impress her with the importance of the issue.

Have Regular Meetings for Ongoing Training and Good Communication

There is little else to talk about here that I didn't cover in the previous section, but I would certainly like to restate that you should meet often, probably every two or three days at first, until the assistant is thoroughly familiar with your unique style; then you should meet once a week to talk about the past week and the week ahead. It is simply good business to communicate effectively and often.

Changing Old Habits

There can sometimes be a downside to hiring an experienced agent as an assistant. Many agents who leave the lending or brokerage businesses do so because they developed bad work habits, such as procrastination, telephone fright, poor time planning, and other issues. If you see any of these negative habits appearing, you have an

You are going to have to open his head and yank out the old bad habits and put in the new ones.

interesting task ahead of you. You are going to have to open his head and yank out the old bad habits and put in the new ones, and then close his head again so that he can operate properly, much as you would do with a machine that had malfunctioned.

Often it takes only a short meeting and is a minor issue, but if he continues to be messy, is habitually late for work, can't seem to get organized, or won't create or adhere to a systematic way of doing things, then you are left with no alternative but to sever your relationship with him. This is very unfortunate, but it is a part of being the boss; just be sure that you are fair, that you have given him ample notice of the required changes, and let your business mind rule over your emotions in the way that you handle the issue.

How to Effectively Work with Your Licensed Assistant

Make Him or Her Feel Like an Important Part of Your Team

Can you think of even one person who likes to work at a job where he or she is shown no appreciation and has no input as to how to make it more efficient?

Can you think of even one person who likes to work at a job where he or she is shown no appreciation and has no input as to how to make it more efficient? Of course not, and I can't either.

We all want to work at a job where we are empowered to direct what goes on and make it more efficient. Almost all of us really like it when someone takes the time to show genuine appreciation for the work that we do.

Do you remember the last time that you got a thank-you letter from a satisfied client, telling you what a great job you did for them? Sure, we all do, and your new assistant is no different, so be sure to thoroughly train her in the new position, then empower her to look for ways to make your operation even better. Watch how she responds and you will be pleasantly surprised at what you see.

If she gives you a suggestion that just doesn't make sense to you, or that you don't understand, ask her to explain to you in detail how that suggestion will benefit your operation, including an explanation of any downside to the idea. If you don't like the idea, hear her out completely while taking notes. Then "suggest" what it is that troubles you or makes you uncomfortable about the suggestion and ask her if she has a solution that will make it work for you. She might just surprise you and come up with a viable new idea that will make your operation even better. If not, simply thank her and tell her that you will take it under consideration. Don't ever belittle her or make her feel stupid as this is a sure way to lose an assistant and stifle any initiative to help you grow your operation.

Ask her opinion about ideas that you have. As she matures as a result of handling your clients and customers and overseeing your escrows or loan files, she will be able to give you an excellent perspective on new ideas and initiatives that you come up with. You will often be very pleased with her viewpoint of your ideas.

It is a good idea to remember birthdays and anniversaries as this goes a long way toward making your assistant feel like a valued member of your team. A small gift and even lunch, if you have the time, is a wise investment in a valued team member.

Good Communication Is a Must

You have transitioned from an individual operation, with your thoughts and ideas harbored in your own mind, to a team of two or more people, each with his or her own thoughts, ideas, and opinions about the real estate or lending world around you. You need to make the most of this. You probably have more talent than you realize and if you have regular meetings with good, open, and honest communication, you will greatly enhance the effectiveness of your operation.

If you have regular meetings with good, open, and honest communication, you will greatly enhance the effectiveness of your operation.

When you first hire your new assistant you should plan on meeting every day for a few weeks. This will help the two of you get used to each other and you will both learn how to communicate better with each other. Your assistant will also learn how to better communicate with other people on your behalf as he gets to know you and how you work.

After a few weeks, you will probably find that a weekly meeting is all that is normally necessary in order to maintain excellent communication. This may be more realistic for real estate agents than for lenders as a loan file can often change more dramatically from day to day than an escrow file. Just be sure to err on the side of too many meetings rather than too few because this makes for better communication between you and your assistant.

The effectiveness of your meetings will be enhanced if you have a written agenda. Your assistant can make up the agenda a day or two prior to your usual meeting day, with input from you about items that you want to discuss, as well as items that he feels are important to talk about. Be sure that the agenda is distributed to all team members the day prior to the meeting so that everyone involved can review it and put together some thoughts for any items that they feel need addressing.

Many lenders simply bring all current loan files to the meeting and review each one of them. Then they discuss any upcoming advertising or marketing that is being formulated or about to be launched and any other operational issues that are important to the effective running of their teams. Many real estate agents do the same thing with their escrow files and current listings.

I know one mortgage broker who uses a checklist in his meetings. He has a huge operation with well over 100 loans going at any given time. He uses the checklist as he goes over each loan in progress, including the after-closing thank you letter.

> *When it comes to communication, the old adage that "more is better than less and sooner is better than later" is very, very true.*

When it comes to communication, the old adage that "more is better than less and sooner is better than later" is very, very true.

Delegate Everything Possible and Create a Daily Work Schedule

This is at the very core of why you elected to hire an assistant in the first place. Your interest in this book shows that you have grown your business to a point where *you* simply aren't enough

> *Delegate everything possible and create a daily work schedule.*

to maintain your business in the way that it should be maintained to grow and prosper further.

We have already talked in some detail about creating new job descriptions for you and for your assistant; now it is time to implement each of them. After training your assistant thoroughly, you will need to put your trust in him more and more as time goes by. Remember, your main activity has now become *lead generation*, and you must immediately start to plan your time and your activities in such a manner that you are in contact with as many new leads per day as possible. Don't be surprised if this new role feels a bit strange at first and actually feels similar to the anxiety that you felt as a new real estate or loan agent with a lot of time on your hands.

Delegate everything that you can to your assistant. Are you starting to get the picture here about how important his telephone presence is going to be?

In all probability, you will refine your mutual job descriptions several times as your new team evolves. You will tend to delegate more and more duties to your assistant as he matures into the new position and proves himself to you while you become better and more effective at pursuing the various ways of meeting new clients.

For the first month or two, don't be surprised if you find yourself doing things that you have delegated to your assistant; it's just human nature at work. We humans do not like change and are often uncomfortable with it to a greater or lesser degree.

The important thing is to be aware of what you are doing on a day-to-day basis and learn to adjust as you go along. An open discussion with your new assistant about this and your changing roles right in the beginning will serve you both very well.

While you are in the process of hiring an assistant, but prior to actually doing so, take the time to sit down and create a daily work schedule for your assistant. I highly recommend that you plan out her entire first month in advance. It is, of course, subject to change as you go along, but setting it in writing has two benefits: It will benefit the assistant by giving her a very clear picture of what her duties are and what your work habits are. She will begin to formulate her own pattern of effectively handling all of the details of her position much sooner than if they are thrown at her piecemeal and often at the last minute.

You will benefit from this type of planning because it will force you to analyze each duty or task and decide who does it. It will let you move many things to the assistant's job description and find out just how much valuable time you really do have now to create more new business.

This type of planning is the very essence of what is known as *time compression.* The effective use of an assistant by delegating everything possible lets you literally compress time by being able to see more people and do more lead generating activities in any given day than you ever could have done without one.

> **This type of planning is the very essence of what is time compression.**

After you have created the entire first month's daily work schedule, you should take the time each week to set a schedule for your assistant for the following week. This probably does not need to be as detailed as the first month's schedule was since the everyday tasks have already been established. You will need only to be sure that she is aware of any noteworthy issues that will take place that week, such as mailings, closings, updating your database, and other issues that do not always happen every week.

Set a Clear Standard of Care and Enforce It

The essence of what you and your operation are about is how well you take care of your clients and customers. If they enjoyed the experience they'll be back, and they will refer their friends and family; if they didn't like the experience, they won't be back—period.

Depending on how familiar your new assistant is with the real estate or lending business, you will have to carefully describe what you do and the level at which you do it. But it is just as important to be sure that your assistant fully understands *why* you work at such a high level of customer satisfaction.

Remember, the main source of new assistants is agents who, for one reason or another, opted out of the real estate brokerage or lending business and people who have never worked in a service industry before. They probably do not realize the importance of each and every satisfied client as it relates to your income and your reputation, so you must carefully indoctrinate them as to the high level of service that you give to your customers and clients and emphasize that you expect the same performance from your assistant.

My dentist is an example of what I mean here. He is not only an excellent technician, he is a highly astute businessman. Every person on his staff, from the front office people to the hygienist to the assistant who puts that goop in your mouth to take impressions, is well trained to make your visit a very pleasant one. They greet you by name when you arrive, they are pleasant and engage you in conversation whenever possible during your visit, and they thank you for coming as you pay your bill and leave. That dentist is a man who knows the true essence of building a team. He has had the same five ladies working for him for several years in a business that is rife with turnover.

Setting a clear standard of conduct and work ethic has meaning only if you enforce it. Hiring an assistant is often the first time that a real estate or loan agent is put into the position of being a boss.

Setting a clear standard of conduct and work ethic has meaning only if you enforce it.

People do not always have the same viewpoint of what a high professional standard of client representation is, and this can be a source of friction between you and your assistant. It is really no different from what I face every day as a branch manager of a real estate office, magnified many times.

The obvious issue is that you must present a crystal clear picture of what you expect and why. Hiring someone and giving him only a vague idea of how you operate, then expecting him to adhere to some lofty ideal that he knows nothing about is a sign of poor leadership and it is sure to create friction almost immediately.

A person cannot be held to a standard if he doesn't know what the standard is; however, if you have done your job correctly and your assistant, who is thoroughly trained as to what you represent and how you work, does not meet your standard, you must then become the enforcer.

You can use various ways to gain acceptance and adherence to your standards. The most effective is through good supervision and an open dialogue in a business-level tone of voice. If your assistant does not respond to your "business-neutral" corrections and directions, then it is time for a private talk during which you must be as stern as you feel that you need to be.

This meeting will be more beneficial to you both if you stay as calm as possible when you bring up the behavior that is not acceptable. Address each issue in full, explain what it is that you find intolerable, explain what it does to hurt your organization, and ask why he has persisted in doing it. This will sometimes bring out things that you had no idea were going on, such as personality conflicts with others in your office or on your team, trouble at home, financial difficulties, and many other issues.

If you encounter problems such as these, it is your job to offer any suggestions that you have that may ease the situation, but you must also tell the person that the offending behavior must stop or you will have to let him go. This is not easy to do, but if you don't do it—and I mean sooner rather than later—your reputation and that of your entire operation will suffer the consequences.

If after whatever you feel is a sufficient number of "attitude adjustment" meetings your assistant still has not responded to your required changes, then it is time to sever him from your team. Hopefully, you have operated under an "at-will" contract that specifies that either of you can terminate the contract with thirty days written notice, and that you may terminate it immediately for "cause."

While you may be able to sever your relationship with an unsatisfactory assistant right away, it may be best to keep a log of the offending activities, such as habitually coming to work late, excessive sick days, angry client calls, and so forth as soon as you begin to sense a problem. That way, you will have a log of the offending activities and your meetings to correct them that went unheeded. If your former assistant decides to go to an attorney to file a wrongful termination suit, you have covered yourself very well. Be sure to check with your own attorney about this matter as labor relation issues differ somewhat from state to state.

The Five Deadly Sins, or How to Lose a Good Licensed Assistant

Praise in Public, Criticize in Private

We have talked a lot here about your standards and being sure that your new assistant is made aware of them. Few things motivate continuing excellent work from an assistant more than sincere praise for a job well done. Just about all of us have a desire to do well at our jobs and to be recognized for it, even in some small way.

Real estate and mortgage brokerage careers are not easy ones, and I never miss a chance to give sincere praise to the agents who work for me when they have done an excellent job. When I do congratulate someone, I am always careful to do it in front of some of the other agents or the administrative staff in the office since this gets double mileage. The agents are very happy to receive a nice compliment from me and they are doubly pleased to receive it in front of their peers. Actually, it makes me feel good, too!

From a management standpoint, publicly recognizing good behavior is the surest way to reinforce it in an induvidual's mind and to get him or her to repeat it over and over again, so never miss a chance to publicly praise those who work for you. I would caution you to be sincere about it, however, or it will lose all meaning.

When someone who works for you does something that offends you or even just irritates you, it is time for the two of you to go to your office or a conference room or any place that is private and have a talk. You should never redress that person in public; that is the fastest way I know of to lose an employee and it simply isn't the right thing to do. It is a rare human being who will never make a mistake, including you and me. When someone who works for you does make one, you will certainly hurt far more than help by embarrassing him or her in public. The first time that you do it, you will change your relationship with that person forever; it will never be quite the same. Whether that individual does stay with you depends solely on how thick-skinned he or she is.

There is a distinct difference between a simple mistake or omission and gross negligence, and you are bound to react to the latter far more emotionally than the first. However, the public forum is not the place for any discussion about it; you simply cannot do that.

No matter how vexing the problem is, take the time to collect all of the facts first, get both sides of the story, calm down, and let your immediate anger pass before setting the *private* meeting. After you have heard your assistant's side of the story you can evaluate the situation and take the positive steps necessary to either correct the situation or do whatever damage control is necessary.

No matter how vexing the problem is, take the time to collect all of the facts first.

I know an agent who simply overloaded herself with too much work, and too much financial responsibility, both personally and in her business. She hired too many people who were hangers-on and were not accountable to her. About two years of this took its toll on her emotionally and physically. She began to show signs of stress-related illness and she became short-tempered and even publicly abusive to her assistant, who is one of the best in the area. The assistant, who had been with her for years and was very instrumental in helping her build her business by millions of dollars, endured the abuse for several months and then resigned. The assistant was immediately hired by someone else. The only winner in that situation was the second agent. Don't let that happen to you as good assistants are very much worth keeping.

Your Bad Day Is Yours, Not Theirs

Working at the upper echelons of a real estate or lending career is a time consuming, demanding job—that's a given. A good licensed assistant will only serve to make it better for you.

Your bad day is yours, not theirs.

Although this is an absolute fact, it has puzzled me for many years as to why so many agents will use their assistants as dumping grounds for every little bit of trauma that comes their way and then be devastated when their assistants finally leave. This isn't rocket science, it's human behavior that we're talking about here. The Golden Rule is alive and well! If you don't like being set upon or treated rudely by someone don't do it to those around you, including your assistant.

The ridiculous demands from the buyers on that expensive listing of yours, the low appraisal on that expensive home that you are doing the loan on, or the fact that your spouse was a real jerk this morning is your problem—and *only* your problem. It's probably all right to mention these things to your assistant since you probably do have a close relationship, but to come to the office and start to find things to pick at him or her about because you are in a bad mood is just not right and will ultimately cost you a very valued employee.

Expect Excellence, but Train Thoroughly

We talked about this somewhat earlier in another context, but it bears looking at in more detail here. Your personal and business reputation is the ultimate

Expect excellence, but train thoroughly.

shining star that attracts clients to you and retains them. Whenever you hire another person to work for you she can either elevate or detract from your reputation, so you have the right to expect her to be nothing less than a true asset to you and your business. However, it is totally your responsibility to show her *in detail* what your version of excellence is. You have a duty to give your new assistant good, thorough, initial training and to follow up with ongoing training and guidance.

Let's look at an example. Suppose that you have been at the top of your game and doing very well in the luxury home market and your assistant is very in tune with your mailings and other marketing issues. You decide that you are going to expand your income by marketing small apartment houses as well. You get a list of apartment house owners from your favorite title company and decide to do a series of mailings to those owners. You assume that your assistant will create your brochures for you as she always does for the luxury homes. Can you see the problem looming on the horizon?

Your assistant knows nothing about marketing apartment houses and doesn't have the faintest idea about what information to put in a brochure to make it attract buyers and please sellers. You list an apartment house and the owners are expecting an attractive brochure to appear in a few days, so you give your assistant a copy of the listing as you always do and ask her to "do her stuff." She misses the mark on several important sales features and benefits and the brochure is generally lacking; you are disappointed and angry and tell her so. She is now angry and frustrated at you for not properly training her about the finer points of what is important to buyers of apartment houses. Can you see how only a few instances like this would tend to make an otherwise loyal assistant start to look elsewhere?

Proper Pay and Reasonable Bonuses Bring Big Dividends

As stated in Chapter 1, at this writing the average hourly rate of pay for a licensed assistant is between $11 an hour for a newly licensed assistant with no experience, to as much as $20 an hour plus a bonus program for a highly experienced veteran with years of experience and wonderful people skills. Some agents, such as Debbie Storms-Green, whom you will meet in Chapter 10, pay their assistants a flat percentage of their gross income. Both of these methods of compensation have merit.

The salary-plus-bonus system and the percentage-of-gross-income system provide for a performance-based reward system for excellence. My wife, Eileen, whom you will meet in Chapter 11, receives a financial bonus for every million dollars that her employer closes each month, so it is in her best interest to help her employer be as proficient as she can be. She is usually handling all of the escrow work for about twenty-five to just under thirty escrows at any given time.

An assistant who is paid a percentage of the agent's gross income has a built-in incentive program as well. The more that his employer makes in commissions, the more he makes, so he, too, wants to keep his employer as sharp and productive as possible.

An assistant who is paid a percentage of the agent's gross income has a built-in incentive program as well.

A trouble spot for agents who are going to hire new assistants is that they often find it difficult to part with those hard-earned commission dollars, so they tend to offer too little pay or incentives to attract good help.

Don't be cheap here—it will hurt you!

Keep the Workload Reasonable to Avoid Burnout

Once you have hired and thoroughly trained your new assistant, you will start to see an increase in the number of listings that you take and purchase contracts that you write.

There is a fine line between getting maximum efficiency from your assistant and overworking her to the point of burnout. Watch carefully for signs of stress, such as health issues, an increase in absenteeism, a negative attitude, complaints from your clients about her attitude over the phone, and any negative change in behavior.

Assistants are the backbone of a successful agent's business and they know it. They are loyal to a fault and will often just continue to try to cope with the additional workload instead of communicating to you that it may be time to reevaluate the size of the team. The additional stress that this causes can be intense and if you don't stay very aware of it, you could easily lose a terrific assistant.

8

Operational Issues

Create Systems and Use Them

*W*hether you work alone or have a team of several members, you will work far more efficiently if your business is systematized. Any reasonably successful agent will tell you that when we create business, we create chaos. The only way to cope with it effectively is by *systematically* handling as many of the tasks and details as we can. The purpose of this book is to encourage you to have your assistant handle as many of the systematized tasks as possible, leaving you free to create new business.

Most of the large real estate companies and lenders operating today have checklists that their employees and agents must follow. In the real estate business it is often called the "homework sheet" or "property verification form." The lenders must send out the "Good Faith Estimate of Settlement Costs" in a timely manner.

These types of forms have appeared on the scene the same way that most changes and additions to the purchase/sale transaction have—as a result of ever-higher expectations by buyers and sellers regarding full disclosure issues and the resulting litigation that has taken place as a result of these expectations.

There has never been a time in recent history when we, as real estate and lending professionals, have had to be more careful and thorough about how we interact with the consumer. You must see that your assistant is thoroughly trained on every system that you and your company have available, and that he or she uses them appropriately.

The surest way to meet your customer's needs, to see that they have all of the information that they need, to keep your company happy with you about your paperwork, and to protect you and your company from litigation is to have systems in place that automatically help you handle every issue that is your responsibility.

When you are marketing a home for someone via a listing agreement, you must address several issues, such as the following:

- Installing and removing "For Sale" and "Sold" signs,

- Installing and removing the keysafes,

- Deciding how often to advertise, and where,

- Determining how often to call the owners,

- Completing the Written Disclosure Statement,

- Verifying everything from the school system to the zoning to the size of the lot or acreage and the square footage of the structure.

In addition to these, a multitude of other disclosure issues occur during the escrow period, such as the ability of the buyers to obtain property insurance, the presence of mold, analyzing the home inspection report, advising your clients on concerns that they have, and so forth.

The real issue with the items listed and others in an average escrow or loan is not just seeing to the timely dissemination of information—it is sometimes more important to be able to prove that you gave the information to the client or customer in a timely manner. Nothing will help to make you popular with your clients and protect you better than a systematized way of obtaining and giving information, and being able to prove that you did so. If you don't have some sort of checklist then you should make one as soon as possible.

If you don't have some sort of checklist then you should make one as soon as possible.

A word of caution here: Both you and your assistant should keep some form of communication log with every loan or sale file. For those of you who are out and about in your cars during the day, I recommend that you purchase a small handheld digital recorder to keep with you. While you are away from your desk and your files, you can make quick verbal notes into it about anything that has taken place during your day that should be logged into your file, and then you can transcribe all of the items at a later time when you are in the office.

I started doing this many years ago and it has paid big dividends in client satisfaction and as a way of helping people to recover from "selective memory" when they conveniently forget something that was said to them.

Appendix C of this book contains sample escrow checklists that you may use or alter in any way that works for you.

Client Contact: Methods, Frequency, and Groups

There are two things to talk about when we address client contact: current *and* past clients. To ignore either one is to lose valuable business, and possibly your reputation.

New and current clients who are house hunting or are already in escrow or have applied for a loan feel a need to have almost daily contact. This can take an immense amount of your time away from other more productive activities, and yet their concerns and need for information are valid.

This is definitely an area where your assistant can be of tremendous help. By creating a simple form to use each day to remind him which clients need an update call or e-mail, he can systematically contact your new and newer clients for you and make them feel secure and well-cared for.

Your past clients are an immensely valuable resource for repeat and referral business and they should be treated as such. If you are like me, many of your best friends started out as clients; that's one of the real rewards of this business.

In my second book, *How to Become a Mega-Producer Real Estate Agent in Five Years*, I talk about how important it is for you to have a well-documented database of your past clients. All clients that you wish to maintain a relationship with should be in your database and the information needs to be kept current. Each time that you talk to a past client and find out about the new baby or grandchild or the new pet, get the details and have your assistant update your database immediately. The database should also include past clients' addresses and phone numbers, any rental property that they own, and the dates that they bought them.

There are many methods of contacting your clients. We have already covered having your assistant call or e-mail some or all of your current clients regularly with escrow or loan updates. Your past clients need to hear from you regularly as well. The real estate and lending businesses are definitely an "out of sight, out of mind" business and unless you are in fairly constant contact with your past clients they are likely to forget you, and that could be costly.

> *The real estate and lending businesses are definitely an "out of sight, out of mind" business.*

Several effective ways to contact your past clients include personal visits, telephone, mail, and e-mail. In order to determine who is best-suited to contact your clients—you or your assistant—it will be necessary for you to segment your database. You do this by looking at each client individually and deciding whether he or she is an A, B, C or D client, and then assigning that client to a category. Let's take a look at each one and see whether you or your assistant is best suited to make the contact.

The As are your very best clients; they are the "givers" of the world who really like helping other people and have already referred people to you. They are the ones that you will pay the most attention to. Your A clients should receive a mailing from you every month, without fail. This can obviously be handled by your assistant, with guidance from you as to what to send. After awhile, your assistant will get as proficient at selecting "items of value" to send to your clients as you are and she can handle the whole thing with minimal review by you.

In addition to the monthly mailings, you should personally visit your A clients. This is time well spent as it leads to new referrals on a consistent basis and is certainly not something that you would have your assistant do.

The Bs are people who haven't yet given you a referral, but you think that once you have indicated to them several times that you would really appreciate their referrals, they would become As and start referring people to you. You should mail to these people every month as well, but call them only every two or three months (remember to check the Do-Not-Call list). The mailings can be handled very efficiently by your assistant, but you should make the calls personally.

The Cs are people you have sold to or know, whom you just can't figure out. They know you, but you just don't know if they will ever refer anyone to you or even use your services again in the future (you know the ones that I'm talking about—the people who are always shopping around for the lowest loan fee or the lowest commission, and little else seems to matter).

These are people whom you want to maintain some contact with as they can sometimes surprise you. You should only mail to them. You will have to make a personal decision about how often to mail to them, but every four to six months seems to be what I hear the most from the high-producing pros out there. This can obviously be handled completely by your assistant with minimal supervision from you.

You will want to delete D clients and customers. These are people who were or are too demanding, have an agent in the family, etc., and have no reason to work with you, or you don't want to work with them any longer.

Sorting people into groups can be a very effective way of communicating with them about special interests that they have, especially by e-mail. If, for instance, you have several dog owners in your database, you can be on the lookout for articles and news about dog shows, new breeds, and even specials on dog food at the local supermarket. Call up this group from your e-mail list and send them relevant information that you find. They really seem to appreciate it! Your assistant can easily be trained to do this sort of thing for you, but you can both be on the lookout for good "stuff."

A word of caution: When you e-mail any group in your database, be sure to e-mail to yourself and "BCC" or blind copy your group. It is considered Internet courtesy not to splash people's e-mail addresses around. To do this, open a new e-mail and the "To" box, the "CC" box, and the "BCC" box will appear at the upper left of the new e-mail screen. Put your e-mail address in the "To" box and put your client group in the "BCC" group. They will receive a message addressed to you and will come to associate it with timely information about something unique to them. They will always open your e-mails, and they will appreciate your thoughtfulness in not sending their e-mail addresses to a bunch of strangers.

Finally, a word about the National Do-Not-Call list: Do not take this lightly. This is serious stuff and can get you in hot water. There are strict rules about whom you can call and huge fines if you are reported and found to be in violation of the law. If you haven't already become fully informed about this law, please do so at once because it's that serious!

After-Hours Calls and Inquiries

Although there are many benefits to having an assistant, one of the major ones is being able to create an "on-call" schedule with your assistant. It's no secret that in the real estate brokerage and lending businesses, new, current, and past clients call you after hours. These calls are often the source of referrals and new inquiries that bring in revenue. Many times you have just put in a nine- or ten-hour day for the eighteenth straight day and you've had enough; you just need to rest. The last thing that you want to do is deal with these after-hours phone calls, yet you don't want to lose the revenue. What do you do?

You set up an "on-call" schedule with your assistant so you can rotate taking the after-hours calls. My personal experience as well as my research with several mega-producing agents shows clear evidence that a weekly schedule works out the best. It fits better into vacation schedules and creates a meaningful evening rest period for each of you; one day at a time just doesn't seem to clear the mind enough, but a week does.

Get a calendar and create a schedule for the two of you, or however many assistants you have, and the person who is scheduled for any given week handles all of the after-hours calls for that week. If you have an answering service, you will need to give the service a copy of the after-hours calendar with instructions about how to forward the calls. If you have a digital recorder or voice mail only at night, you will need to remember to change the message each week to reflect the proper person.

Remember, people should not be expected to do something for nothing, so when your assistant is on call, and takes a call that turns into revenue, you should expect to pay him or her on some predetermined basis such as a referral fee of twenty percent of the revenue received or a set dollar amount from each of those closings. Almost all of the agents that I interviewed about this use a percentage referral fee that ranges from twenty to twenty-five percent of the commission earned.

To keep everything aboveboard, create a form that your assistant must submit each morning that lists all inquiries from the preceding evening; that way a call during normal business hours cannot be turned in the next day for the unearned referral fee. Returning calls to people on this form will also be high on your priority list the following morning.

Another issue that you need to be prepared to deal with is when your assistant takes a call from someone who asks for you and won't deal with anyone but you. Should all of these callers be told that you are not available and that you will call them in the morning, or should your assistant have instructions to call you with their names and phone numbers? This issue will come up many times, so prepare for it ahead of time and save your assistant from an uncomfortable situation.

If your assistant takes a call from an after-hours caller who will talk only with you, it is best to pay him a referral fee or set fee for these calls as well. Some agents that I interviewed said that they pay a ten- to fifteen-percent referral fee for these calls.

Weekend and Vacation Coverage

This is where the true value of an assistant shines through like a beacon! We are in a service business, and when you aren't there to give service you are out of business.

This is where the true value of an assistant shines through like a beacon!

There are two ways to cover yourself when you are off for the weekend or on vacation: You can pay another agent in your office or company to handle your business while you are away, which is often a very expensive proposition, or you can have your assistant handle all of your business while you are away and only pay his or her regular salary and maybe a small bonus.

Another nice thing about having an assistant is that you can be away for a two-week vacation but still be fully in business for 52 weeks out of the year.

You can be away for a two-week vacation but still be fully in business for 52 weeks out of the year.

When I was selling for a national real estate company during the mid-nineties, a good friend of mine worked at the same office that I did. He did almost as much business as I did and was as careful about how he did it as I was. We took a similar amount of time off so we used to handle each other's business and we never charged each other anything. It was a great setup.

If you have someone like that in your company or office, you are very fortunate. If not, then you will probably need to negotiate with another agent about what you expect from her and how much she is be paid and for which people. This can become very tedious.

The advantage to having an assistant is that you have trained him or her exactly *your* way and you can relax and rest assured that *your* business will be handled *your* way by *your* licensed assistant, and not by someone that you are not completely sure about.

Weekends are pretty straightforward; you can handle them pretty much as you handle the after-hours calls, usually by simply addressing the issue on your monthly on-call calendar.

Vacations are a little different. If you don't get some time completely away from your business, it has a tendency to devour you. This can lead to burnout, too much stress, and a host of physical and family ailments. Every successful agent has at least a little ego (some have more) that sometimes prevents him from admitting that someone else can do his job just as well as he can. This can often get in the way of good judgment about delegating duties to others.

The people who have the highest quality lives and the most successful businesses are also the best at delegating.

My research, which spans over thirty years, reveals that the people who have the highest quality lives and the most successful businesses are also the best at delegating every aspect of their business to carefully selected, highly competent people when necessary.

I have heard people make light of former U.S. President Ronald Reagan over the years as to his personal abilities. People who deride him really don't stop to consider that due to his wonderful ability to delegate responsibility, he had one of the most successful presidencies in history. If you are going to build and maintain a high-quality business, then you must learn to do the same thing.

It may be tempting to want to "check in" every day while you are sitting on a beach somewhere, but if you do, there is every chance that something will "need" your attention, and your time with your friends or family will certainly be intruded on. Don't fall for this. If you have a capable assistant working for you who is instructed to call you only in the event of an absolute emergency, then your business will most certainly be there waiting for you when you get back.

If you are going to expect your assistant to show property and take listings for you while you are on vacation or during weekends, you will need to cover this issue in the employment interview. Many people become assistants instead of real estate agents or lenders because they do not want to work on the weekends. I recently saw a real estate agent lose a top assistant because she insisted, long after hiring her, that her assistant begin showing property for her when she was away and on weekends.

9

It's a Family Affair: The Husband and Wife Team

Are You Professionally Compatible?

One of the fastest growing partnerships in the real estate industry today is the husband-and-wife team.

One of the fastest growing partnerships in the real estate industry today is the husband-and-wife team. Provided that you are professionally compatible, you have the makings of an excellent and cost-effective team.

After our four children were in high school, my wife, Eileen, worked as an agent, sometimes for one company while I worked as a manager for another and sometimes in the same office that I was in. She didn't really care for the seven-day-a-week routine and when I went back into sales we sat down and talked about each of our strengths. We decided that her real strength was in being a licensed assistant, which she has excelled at to this day.

She can get names and telephone numbers of new clients from an open house like nobody I've ever seen, so she used to hold one open house while I either held another one or showed property on Sundays. When she would get a name, she would tell the people that we worked as a team and "one of us would call them tomorrow evening to follow up." Yes, you guessed it; I made the calls and did the "agent" work. Our sales skyrocketed!

Keep in mind that we have been married for 37 years and have always been best friends. We can do business together every day and still find each other entertaining at night; some people can't.

More than one agent that I have known over the years has brought his or her spouse into the business as a partner only to see sales dwindle and their otherwise happy marriages start to unravel. Fortunately, most ended their partnerships before their marriages failed. It's just not for everyone.

A real estate agent who once worked with me brought his wife in as his partner. She was an absolute beauty, but she was spoiled rotten and very pampered. She lacked the skills that are required to work in a service business like ours and she immediately started to greatly offend all of this poor chap's past and current clients. The couple had a very loud and embarrassing "business meeting" in the office in front of about forty people, during which her husband told her she was fired! By the time this happened, she had offended almost all of us with her arrogance and we gleefully tried to stifle our laughter, although it really wasn't funny. She ended up working for an escrow company for awhile then faded away.

I cite these examples as a word of caution to you to sit down together and really talk about your strengths and weaknesses and whether you both think that it is wise for you to become partners. It can quickly and easily go far beyond just being husband and wife—in either direction.

It can quickly and easily go far beyond just being husband and wife—in either direction.

Who Is Going to Be the Primary Agent with Your Company?

Once you have mutually decided to work as a team, you need to decide how you are going to work. In my case, my wife is best suited as a support person. At those times when I was in sales, with her assisting me we were a highly effective team. I know of many husband-and-wife teams that are very effective with both partners working at sales and just splitting the escrow duties as best suited their schedules.

If you decide to work where one of you is the primary agent and the other one is a support person, you will need to sit down and carefully determine what duties each of you will conduct as the primary course of your day-to-day activities. It is almost always evident that either the husband or the wife is better suited to work as the primary agent, and this isn't usually a hard decision to make. What can be a little harder is deciding what duties each of you will fulfill on a regular basis. My suggestion to you, based on my personal experience, is to make a job description for each of you, especially if one spouse is new to the business and doesn't really know the ropes. Stay fluid about this issue and visit it frequently as you go along. Soon each of your respective strengths will come to the surface and you will be able to fine-tune your business accordingly.

Open Houses–Double Duty or Team Effort?

The husband/wife team can be a very effective method of building a business via meeting new clients at an open house because they have two choices. They can either hold separate open houses and both can have the opportunity to meet people, or they can hold an open house together and meet people.

The main advantage of holding separate open houses is that a team can present homes that are in different price ranges. This gives the team the ability to diversify its buyer pool, thereby making it less vulnerable to a lack of listings in any given price range. If all of your buyers are in one general price range and there is suddenly a lack of new inventory in that price range, you are more or less out of business.

Holding separate open houses also gives the team the opportunity to break into a particular neighborhood, price range (such as the luxury home market), or some other niche market while maintaining its current client base. Of course, it also doubles the team's chances of meeting new clients, especially if one member has an open house that no one comes to.

Conversely, if a husband/wife team holds the same house open, they can often match either of their personalities to the visitors as they come in, and they stand a better chance of getting a new client. My wife and I used to do that at times, especially if I was holding open a listing that we knew would be very well attended. It is amazing how some people would gravitate toward me and some would gravitate toward her, but if the visitor was truly in the market, we seldom failed to get a new client.

Finally, the husband and wife team will enjoy the benefit of "two agents—one pocketbook." As long as they are both licensed, either of them can do the most productive thing for the team at any given moment and every dollar in commission that is generated goes into one pot: That's real earning power!

Finally, the husband and wife team will enjoy the benefit of "two agents— one pocketbook."

10

Conversations with Two Top Agents Who Have Assistants

*I*nterview with Michael Block—
Coldwell Banker Success Southwest,
Tucson, Arizona

Bob Herd's comments are in bold and italicized type.
Michael Block's comments are in regular type.

Q

Michael, you've been the top-selling agent with Coldwell Banker Success Southwest several times, haven't you?

Yes, I started my career in 1978 and I have been with Coldwell Banker since 1990, so I've been here about 14 years.

Q

What did you do prior to your real estate career?

I was at the University of Arizona. I graduated in 1978 with a degree in Journalism. In 1978 I used to be able to write really good ads. My mom was in real estate so I grew up around it and I had a really good basic knowledge of what it was all about.

Q

Is that when you decided on a real estate career?

Yeah, I had just gotten out of college and I took 24 units my senior year so that I could graduate within four years and just be done and

I was weary of working under deadlines and copyrighting issues so I just thought I'd try something non-stressful, like real estate. [Laughter.]

My goal was to make $1,000 a month and $12,000 by the end of the year. I came in in April and by December I had made about $28,000. I thought to myself, this is pretty good!

Tell me about your overall business. What has your sales volume been over the last three to four years?

I think that three years ago I was at about $5–$6 million and that was just me; I did have an assistant that was kind of helping out on a part-time basis back then, just working in the office from Monday through Friday with no set hours.

That's the hard part about hiring an assistant because I didn't know if my volume warranted an assistant and yet I knew that if I wanted to do more business that I would have to hire someone to be in the office doing the work so that I could be out with more buyers and sellers. I was real superstitious. I thought I would jinx my business if I hired an assistant and then we'd sit around and look at each other wondering where the business was.

What happened to your volume after that?

When I hired her, in 2001, my volume went to $10 million. In 2003 we did over $16 million with an average sales price of $270,000.

So that's well over a 60 percent increase in your sales volume in three years. Wow, that kind of increase each year is pretty darn good!

About how many units a year does that mean for you?

I think that last year we did 59 units.

Q *How many hours a week did you work before you had an assistant and, on average, how many do you work now?*

Well, let's see, there's 24 hours in a day times 7 days in a week, so that's what I was doing, and it was pretty nuts! Actually, I'd go home and continue to make calls and I didn't consider it still working, but sometimes I'd look up and it would be nine o'clock at night and I'd say, "Where did the kids go?" My wife said, "They've been in bed for an hour and a half."

Now I try to return calls on my way home in my car, which is about a 20 minute drive from the office. By doing that all of the calls are usually done by the time that I get home.

I was literally working seven days a week. I didn't really want to work every weekend any more. My assistant has four kids and she doesn't want to work every weekend either. I don't know how we do it but we manage to keep all of the clients happy and still get time with the families on the weekends.

We work on the phone on the weekends and sometimes we show homes, but somehow it seems to be just five days a week with minimal weekend work.

Q *Well, that's really what it's all about—balance equals longevity.*

How true, how true.

Q *Does your assistant work as a buyer's rep as well?*

Yeah, that was one thing that I liked about finding this assistant. I started out trying to find someone to just do the paperwork and clerical work. She brings a certain uniqueness to my team. She had a six-year career with a different company, so she has her clients and I have mine; then I give her a number of clients to work with. She really does an excellent job, too. We always have a large number of listings, so I give her almost all of the ad calls and she follows up with them.

Q **When you began your real estate career, did you have a business plan?**

No, my plan was to make $1,000 dollars a month and like what I was doing.

Q **That's funny! Do you have a business plan now?**

I've had business plans in the past, but I'm not a real business-plan-oriented person. It's all in my mind. I know almost to the dollar where we spend our advertising dollars. We know what works and doesn't work at any given time.

My assistant and I meet about twice a week and talk about business. We discuss how many ad calls I have received, how the escrows are going, etc. We mutually stay on top of it all the time.

Q **Do you work a specialty or niche market of any kind?**

Not exactly; I am most comfortable working the east and northeast part of Tucson and my assistant knows the west and northwest areas very well, so we tend to hand off clients to each other in those areas and we give better service that way.

Q **So, the advantage that she brings to you as an assistant is that she has specialized knowledge of another area of Tucson that you don't really know very well, and she has broadly expanded your area of expertise.**

That's exactly right.

Q **Approximately what percentage of your business is listings versus sales?**

Well, I concentrate on listings because listings bring phone calls and phone calls turn into buyers and many of them have homes to sell to buy their next one. I track this carefully each year and I always end up at about 50 percent listings.

Q *Roughly what percentage of your business comes from referrals?*

A lot! For the past two years it has been around 85 percent, and I consider past clients doing business with me again to be referrals.

Q *What about marketing? By marketing, I mean things like* **Tucson Lifestyle** *magazine or other image-building things, not necessarily advertising.*

I'm real bad about that, I guess. I don't really do anything to market myself other than a consistent mailing program to my past and current clients. There is nothing that I do to tell the world that I have been the number one Coldwell Banker agent in Tucson for the last three years in a row. I should, but I don't.

Q *So you don't do anything in a purely marketing sense other than your mail outs, and you just do some advertising?*

Yes, that's right.

Q *What type of advertising do you do? Do you use a Website like* **realtor.com, Homes for Sale** *type magazines, newspapers, and things like that?*

Well yeah, I use *realtor.com*, I have my own Website, I just signed up with *homes.com*, I have *michaelsellstucson.com*, and I usually get a page in one of the magazines.

Q *What about telemarketing? Do you do any type of cold calling?*

None at all, none whatsoever.

Q *That's interesting. This is the third real estate book that I have written and I have interviewed a large number of high-producing agents, some with annual sales exceeding $120,000,000, and only one of them has ever done any type of cold calling.*

Well, when I'm home I don't want to be bothered by a telemarketer so I sure don't want to be the one to be aggravating someone else.

Q *What about a mailing program? Earlier you said that you have a very consistent mailing program.*

Yes, we do a lot of mailing. We send out a newsletter every month to our sphere of influence, which includes past customers, friends, and family. Then there's about 2,700 mailers every month that go to areas that I am farming.

Q *And that mailing goes to the same people all the time?*

Every month—every month without fail.

Q *Michael, will you describe to me what role your assistant plays in helping to maintain your effectiveness in these areas.*

At first she was doing the newsletter, but because she's such an effective buyer's rep, we decided that it was a waste of her time and we have outsourced that job to someone else. All my assistant does is put the mailing labels on, have them run through the postal meter and have them put in the mail.

Q *What percentage of your gross commissions do you spend on marketing and advertising?*

I consistently put 10 to 15 percent of my earnings back in the pot.

Q

*That's about average for a high producer. Do you
have any systems in place to track its effectiveness?*

Yeah, I do. We meet often, usually about a couple of times a week and
we track where each new client or customer came from. It changes
constantly, so we just have to keep on top of it. We always ask the
caller what prompted them to call—an ad, a sign, or what? It also
depends on what type of property we are marketing as well.

Q

*When you decided to hire an assistant, did you
set aside a certain amount of extra money to be
able to pay her until your volume increased due to
her efforts?*

Not really. I mean, all I did was to first decide that it was time to get
one, then both of us just went to work—it worked! Actually, back in
1990 I went to a seminar that was given by Howard Brinton, whom
I really respect, and he told of the high degree of efficiency that there
was in basically duplicating yourself through the use of a good assistant, so I tried it. It worked for awhile, but I really hadn't found the
right assistant at that time.

Q

*When did you know that it was time to get
an assistant?*

When everybody told me. I'm a real "type A" personality and I don't
delegate well so I was just doing it all myself and driving myself crazy.
I bought a laptop computer in 1996 and I thought it would make me
so efficient that I wouldn't need an assistant.

I also bought a tiny handheld recorder to give myself reminders on.
That helped a lot, but it didn't replace having another pair of capable
hands at work, helping me.

*It's interesting that you say that, because in an
earlier chapter in this book I tell the readers that
that's exactly what I recommend, a small pocket*

recorder to carry with them. That way, when you think of something that you have to do, or someone to call later, or something to assign to your assistant at a later time, you can easily hold the thought. It's much safer if you are driving and very efficient.

Q

How did you find your current assistant?

She was working for a competitor as an assistant and she wanted to branch out on her own. We have a mutual friend who is a lender and close friend. He called me and told me about her and that she was interviewing and asked if I would be interested in interviewing her. I had just lost my assistant because she wanted to stay home and be a full-time mom, bless her. I wasn't gonna hire anyone right away, but I had heard that she was very capable, so I called her, we met and she was perfect for the needs of my business. She has become a real asset to me. We just celebrated our second anniversary last month. She told me, but I didn't know.

Q

Describe the process that you use to interview— what you found out before and during the interview and how you went about hiring her.

Well, I had a little bit of experience because I had a full-time assistant for about a year and a half before she decided to be a stay-at-home mom, so I went to a very experienced licensed assistant here in our office and I asked her for a checklist of the things that she does that really are helpful to a high-producer like me. Since I wanted a combination buyer's rep as well as a licensed assistant, I asked a lot of questions about how she works, what she does for the person that she's working for and things like that. It turned out to be a great way to find out what she was all about.

There was a time last year when we sold 35 homes in three months so at one point I asked her if she thought we ought to hire a licensed assistant because we were hardly in the office at all. She said that I was the team leader and I could do what I want, but she still wanted to keep things just like they were and keep doing the things in the office. I can see, though, that we are going to have to add to the team soon because she is so effective at selling homes that she is better utilized in that position.

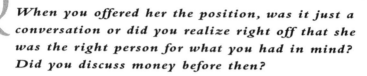

When you offered her the position, was it just a conversation or did you realize right off that she was the right person for what you had in mind? Did you discuss money before then?

I asked her right up front what she was currently making and she told me what her income was and that she was working way too hard to only make that much. I knew her by reputation and I felt certain that she could add sufficiently to my sales volume to pay her $35,000 to $40,000 dollars a year, plus she would make even more in commissions from the business that I would give to her, not to mention the business that she generated on her own. She brought a $500,000 buyer over with her when she came and she got the lion's share of that.

So, do you guys meet regularly?

Yeah, we are in the office five days a week, and we always take the time to talk about her business and my business and how we can help each other. We also go into a conference room with all of the files and go over each one. By getting out of my office, we can get away from the phone and other distractions and concentrate on the work at hand. It also gives me a chance to tell her what I would like for her to do and what needs to be done.

And you do that once a week?

We try to do it at least once a week. It's hard sometimes because we are just so busy, but it's important enough to the smooth running of the operation that we stick very close to that schedule. There are times when we will have, like, 16 sales in a month and we barely have time to look at each other, but we still make time to review everything.

Q **What type of training did you give your assistant?**

I don't know that I gave her any type of formal training. She came to me as a very experienced person that was really up to speed on how to make things happen the right way. I did train her on the peculiarities of the way that I work, and that didn't take much time. That's the reason that I pay her as much as I pay her, because she brings so much to the table. She is a female version of me and that has been such a blessing to me. Some of my clients would rather work with her than me and that's fine with me.

Q **You know, when I was in sales, my wife worked with me the same way and it was an incredibly effective team; she was the same way and the client could always feel comfortable with one of us!**

Yeah, I really like that part of it.

Q **Do you have a written contract with her?**

I don't have a written contract with her. She came to me with a written job description, we edited it and I gave her some additional duties and deleted some things. We finalized that document and mutually agreed that we would try it for a six-month trial period; that was 25 months ago and we haven't looked at it since.

About eight months into it my assistant said that we never did have our six-month review. I am not detail-oriented like that, so I just said that I thought she was doing a great job and that I felt that it was working out very well. I asked her if she was getting out of it what she wanted and she said absolutely, and I said, "OK, we just had our review."

Q **Does she work as an independent contractor or as an employee?**

She works as an independent contractor. At one point I hired my mother-in-law as an employee. It worked out all right, but I wasn't as satisfied with it as I thought I would be. She really didn't want to come into the office. She wanted to work at home and just do the newsletter and things like that. I found that, to be really effective, an assistant needs to be in the office, working under the same roof.

Q

Have you created any forms or checklists that you and your assistant use for greater efficiency?

Yes, I think that it's important to the effective running of the team. Some of them serve mainly as a reminder of things that need to be done in each escrow and they really help us to stay on track and get things done in a timely manner. They are very informal and are "don't forget to do these things" kinds of forms.

Q

Would you mind if I share that one particular form with our readers?

Sure, I'll make you a copy. It's pretty crude and elementary.

Those are the ones that work.

Q

How do you work it with your assistant to cover for you after hours and when you are on vacation?

That's the best part of having an assistant. I was joking with you earlier about working 24/7. Awhile back I took the family out of town on three separate occasions and I didn't have coverage at all. I was uncomfortable about it and it wasn't a good thing. Now, I leave town and it's great because my assistant just takes over. I'll leave her a whole bunch of voice mail messages the night before I leave. She takes it and handles it so well and I can just go and I never have to worry about everything going smoothly while I'm away. For instance, I'm leaving shortly to attend the Coldwell Banker International Business Conference in Las Vegas. It's a problem this time since my assistant is going with me and my family, so we'll both have to stay very close to the voice mail and cell phone.

Normally, we both schedule out-of-town stuff and vacations at least six months out with each other so that there are no last minute surprises. I have four out-of-town trips scheduled between now and the end of May and it's nice to know that I can just leave town and I just forward my phone to her. I trust her very much and it's very comforting.

Q *What programs or methods do you have in effect to retain past clients and receive referrals and repeat business from them?*

Twenty years ago I would sell a home to someone and I didn't have any real follow-up system. Then I would see a client of mine in the grocery store or someplace like that and they would tell me that their mom just moved into town and bought a home; that hurt!

What I have in place now is a systematic mailing program where all of my current and past clients get something in the mail from me at least once a month. They are all designed to keep me a household name and to *gently* remind them that I appreciate their repeat business and their referrals. I'm not comfortable calling and asking for referrals so I let the newsletter do it for me and it works very well.

Q *What does your assistant do to help you retain past clients and get new ones?*

Well, we haven't gotten to the team part yet, and I don't know that we ever will. She has her clients and I have mine and I don't want to intrude on her clients by sending them my newsletter. Essentially, she works on my monthly newsletter and she sees that they are mailed out to all of my clients. She seems to enjoy doing it.

Q *How often do you contact the people in your database—once a month or according to the relationship that you have with them?*

It varies. Every client gets my monthly newsletter, then there are a few clients that have bought two or three homes from me in the past few years. I'll contact them once a week just to say hi and let them know that I care about them.

> **When you send your newsletter out, do you send "just listed" or "just sold" cards or do you have other content in it?**

The newsletter is pretty cool, I think. The front of it has a blurb about me, and then we'll talk about something within the company, then there will be something in there that everyone can use. It is folded, and reads like a book. It will include recently closed sales in their neighborhood. That gets a little expensive since we are farming 14 or 15 different neighborhoods and the printer has to change that page for each one. Pages one, two and four are exactly the same, but page three is different for each neighborhood.

Now, the 500 people in my sphere of influence get a generic newsletter where all four pages are exactly the same.

> **Do you create this whole newsletter yourself each time?**

I create the shell and get all of the articles, and then I give it to someone else to put it all together for me. I check it, and if I don't like the way that a certain page looks then I let her know and she makes the changes and sends it to the printer; that way I spend minimal time on its development, but I still get it done the way that I like it. It's really paid off very well.

> **So you use a second, part-time assistant to do most of the work and then she gives it to you and your full-time assistant to review and approve before it's printed and mailed, right?**

That's exactly right.

> **Let's talk about your assistant now. Please describe what she actually does for you.**

In a larger sense, she gives me the freedom to do what I need to do to work very effectively with clients. She's in the office every day. She handles the phone calls, sets up and maintains the files, writes the ads, and she makes sure that when the company ads come out that all of our listings are included. She just pretty much pulls everything together and fills in the gaps that I create by bringing in new business. She takes pictures of our new listings, meets home inspectors, appraisers, and those kinds of folks.

For instance, tomorrow we have a tour in Tucson Country Club and someone has to be there. She is taking the first half and I'm taking the second half of the time.

My phone rings a lot, and I really don't want everyone going into voice mail if I can help it, but she's here to answer the phones and set things up as they need to be; it's very efficient for me. If I'm gone on vacation, she's in the office all the time and at the end of each day she'll leave me a 10-minute message telling me what took place, what she did, and any important news that I need to hear. I will then call her back and give any directions to her that I feel are necessary, or, if necessary I'll just make the calls myself. What it does is let me be away but still be as involved as I feel is necessary.

That's very good; that's impressive. What hours does she work and what days of the week?

She works pretty much from 8:30 a.m. until about 4:30 or 5:00 p.m. Monday through Friday. She is also very accommodating about rearranging her weekend schedule to help me with showings in the northwest side of town. That's a real plus because in the past I've had assistants who have said, "I'm sorry, but I can't do that," and then I had to ask myself, "What's the use in having an assistant?" I try not to have that type of thing happen very often as it is an intrusion on her time.

Yes, I've seen that happen, where an agent abuses the delegation process with an assistant to the point that the assistant gets fed up and quits. In fact, that happened to my wife awhile back. It was terrible. So, basically it's an eight-to-five kind of thing with some weekend duty as needed.

Q

How do you compensate her? Salary, hourly wage, referral fees, or what?

I give her a percentage of all of the commissions that I receive; she gets a flat percentage of everything. For business that I refer to her, she gets a higher split, then for business that she brings in herself, she gets a full 50 percent.

She goes out on listing presentations with me so that she can learn the dialogue and the things that are important to discuss with a client. Overall, at the end of last year, I think that she made a little over $100,000.

Wow, that's impressive!

Q

Several agents that I have talked to pay their assistant a flat 10 percent of their gross income; are you about there?

Yeah, exactly. That's right where I am as well.

Q

And she is an independent contractor, not an employee, is that correct?

That's right.

Q

How about company support. How much office space do you and your assistant occupy?

We have one of the bigger offices here, which you can see isn't nearly enough. As you can see, we are very tight in here. This office is about nine feet by nine feet and we have actually spilled over into one of the work stations out in the main office where we keep a lot of our files. I keep the previous years' files there and take the rest home and put them in a storage shed.

Q *So, you have a cubicle out there in the office?*

That's right.

Q *Does the company provide any assistance to you or your assistant over and above the normal type of things?*

Yes, our company has a couple of programs. If you are on a traditional split, the company will pay from $325 to $650 a month more or less as matching funds for a licensed assistant. I don't use that commission split so I don't get that, but it's fine because the split that I am on works out better for me. I pay the company and they turn around and pay her and do the bookkeeping.

Q *Give me some of your opinions and viewpoints. Doing the very high sales volume that you do each year clearly sets you apart from the average salesperson. What do you do that is so different from them?*

I don't know—I really don't! I showed another company's listing to a buyer a few weeks ago. The seller was home when I showed it. A short time later the seller called me and said that she had fired her agent and she wanted me to be her new listing agent. She said that she really liked my enthusiasm when I showed it. I guess I would have to say that it might be my love for the business and my enthusiasm.

Q *I have found that running "narrow and deep," that is, really having saturation-knowledge of a smaller segment of the market clearly sets you apart. Does your assistant help you to achieve this level of knowledge and ability to serve the clients better?*

Absolutely! The plan that we have for full-city coverage with a real in-depth knowledge is that I really have an intimate knowledge of the foothills and the northeast and she has the same knowledge of the west and northwest parts of town.

You asked me earlier what sets me apart from the average agent; I think that it's the degree that we really care about our clients. We don't want to be a "mill," where we have 100 listings and hope that 70 of them sell. I can't have that; I'm too much of a perfectionist. I want every listing of ours to sell.

Q

So, basically she provides escrow services and things of that nature that free your time up and she also provides a greater depth and knowledge of a larger area for you.

Right. I read a long time ago that the ultimate role of the assistant is to free me up to meet with more buyers and sellers; that's the ultimate value that she brings to me. The everyday chores involved in servicing a listing or an open escrow file are very important if you want to keep the client for the future. I need to stay close to those issues, but now I can have my assistant do almost all of them, and because I have introduced her to my clients, they feel just as good as if I were personally doing those things. When you have that, that's when you know that you have really arrived as a team.

I heard of one agent who wrote a $10,000 check to his assistant and told her that if they reached their goal by year-end that he would sign it and she could cash it. I don't feel that it's necessary to do that; I want my assistant to have real pride in her work and in what our mutual reputation is out there. My assistant does that and she gets paid very well for it, too.

Q

In your opinion, what's the single biggest benefit that you bring to your clients?

It changes, but I would say that it's the depth of our knowledge and the degree that we care about them and we let it show. It's definitely the degree of caring.

Q

Is your ability to deliver this benefit to your clients enhanced at all by your assistant?

Absolutely! She allows me to duplicate myself and create millions of dollars worth of additional business without lowering the standard of care that I both want to give and need to give to my clients. She also gives me much more time with my family, and the value of that is immeasurable. In turn, it gives her the ability to do better things for her family as well.

Q *Tell me where you see the residential real estate agent's role in the home or land buying process going in the next several years, and how you see that role enhanced by the use of a licensed assistant.*

Well, I've been hearing for years that we are going to be eliminated because of the Internet. I don't see that at all, in fact I see it as a tremendous benefit to the consumer and to us. People still want a knowledgeable professional on their side when it's time to get serious about acquiring a home and we have never been in such demand as right now. In my opinion, this will continue well into the foreseeable future. The buyers and sellers that come to us now have usually been on the Internet and have a very good knowledge of what it is that they want to accomplish; it's our job to give them the benefit of our enhanced knowledge and negotiating skills to make it happen for them the way that they expect.

The assistant enhances that role by helping with the research and becoming sensitive to the buyer's needs and helping you to deliver what they need. For instance, I sold a home last Friday and the buyers want a survey and every inspection known to man. I called my assistant and told her all about it and she called me on Monday and said that all of the inspections had been ordered and she would be there to let the inspectors in. That really enhances my ability and my relationship with my clients

Q *What are the top three pieces of advice that you can give to a real estate agent who is thinking about hiring a licensed assistant?*

Well, the key is to make sure that they are licensed; do some soul-searching and find out why you feel that you need an assistant and look at your business plan to see where you are now, in terms of production, and where you want to be, and ask yourself if the addition of a licensed assistant will enhance your ability to get there. Additionally, I think that the quality of life issue needs to be addressed as well. It's a huge issue that isn't given enough thought by agents.

Q *What are your thoughts about hiring a licensed versus an unlicensed assistant?*

The problem with unlicensed assistants is: What good are they? They can answer the phone, but then they can't say a whole lot. We already have receptionists here in the office so that's not really a benefit. They can't dispense information, they can't quote prices, they can't hold a home open, they can't put on or take off a keybox, they certainly can't show homes, so really, their usefulness is very limited. I really can't see any real benefit in hiring an unlicensed assistant, but there's a lot of downside. If you do hire an unlicensed assistant and they cross the line in terms of doing any activities that require a license, it could really hurt you.

Q *Is there anything else that you would like to tell the person who is reading this book?*

Well, I think that it's just so very important to find out why you really want to hire an assistant; what's your real goal? Write it out on paper and really analyze it and don't be hasty in hiring someone. Take your time and find someone who is really compatible with you and in tune with what you are all about and where you want to take your business. That person is literally an extension of you every time he or she talks to anyone on your behalf, so be very careful about whom you hire.

*I*nterview with Debbie Storms-Green—
Roy Long Realty Co.,
Tucson, Arizona

Bob Herd's comments are in bold and italicized type.
Debbie Storms–Green's comments are in regular
type.

Debbie, first tell me a little about your background. What did you do prior to your real estate career?

Prior to my real estate career I was an escrow officer with a title company. I started right out of high school. They set me up to be an assistant for an executive secretary for a title company, and I got my first taste of escrow and the real estate business that way. While I was going to the University of Arizona I stayed with the title company part-time and worked as a secretary, then I rolled into being an assistant escrow officer.

I stayed at the U of A for a couple of years and then I really liked the escrow business and became an escrow officer for about seven years, and then I became a real estate agent.

What made you decide on a real estate career?

Partially the escrow side of it was very, very difficult, and it looked to me like the realtors were having a lot more fun than the escrow officers were. My ex-husband's family was in real estate and development, too, and that had an effect on my decision. His dad was a builder and had a lot of real estate for sale and I kinda got into it that way, too.

When did you start in real estate?

I started in 1982.

Twenty-two years—that's a long time!

Q *Tell me a little about your business; what has your sales volume been the last three or four years?*

My sales volume has been at least $10 million a year for the past three years. Actually last year I did less than that, but I normally do at least $10 million in volume every year.

Q *About how many units does that represent a year?*

Gosh, I think that I average about 40 to 50 units a year.

Q *On average, and given changing market conditions, about how much is your sales volume going up each year, or is it staying pretty stable?*

You know what? It goes up as much as I want it to, really. If I want to do more, I do more. I have a strong six-figure income and that's what I want to do, so it stays very consistent.

Q *How many hours a week did you work before you hired an assistant versus now?*

Before I had an assistant, I'm sure that I was working 60 to 70 hours a week. I had to, to keep up with the paperwork and try to do everything that I wanted to do. I still work about 40 hours a week; I don't have to with the assistant, but I do just because I want to. It's my choice now.

Q *When you began your real estate career did you have a business plan, and if you did, how has it evolved over the years?*

I didn't have a business plan, I just jumped into it. You know, I wasn't sure where I was going with the whole thing. I knew that I really liked it but I didn't have a plan. I should have had one; I would have gotten where I wanted to be a lot faster with one.

Q

Do you have one now?

Yes, I do.

Q

Do you work a specialty or niche market, and if you do, can you describe to me what it is and how your assistant helps you to gain or maintain market share in it?

What I prefer is land and home site sales and subdivisions. I will do homes by referral only and I will do buyers by referral only. If someone refers a buyer to me I'll do a great job for them, but I really prefer land and subdivisions.

My assistant, Jessica, helps me by taking areas and sending postcards or letters to people as land listings expire, or if we spot an area where we like the land, she'll send a letter that says that it's a beautiful area and we see that you have a parcel of land there. That's how I get a lot of my land listings. I don't even have to tell her, she does it automatically as a regular part of her job. A lot of times she'll just tell me, "Deb, here's a section that I just mailed to, so in case the people call you, this is what I just sent out." It's something that she does on her own, outside of everything else that we're doing.

It's wonderful because we are trying to target areas where we think the land development is headed. Not just really expensive properties, but land that seems to be in the growth patterns. I want to control that area when the development hits there.

Just by her doing that, I have gotten six listings in the last few months.

Wow, that's amazing!

Q

Approximately what percent of your business is listings versus sales?

Eighty percent of my business is listings.

Q **About what percentage of your listings comes from referrals?**

I would say that at least 30 percent of my business comes from referrals.

Q **Okay. What about marketing? By marketing, I mean image-building stuff like Tucson Lifestyle magazine.**

Probably about 25 percent. I get a lot of calls from ads, though.

Q **How much business do you get from advertising? Stuff like Homes & Land magazine, realtor.com, newspapers, and that sort of thing?**

Right now I have five Websites, so I get a lot of Internet contact, and I mean a lot of it!

Q **Is it mostly local people, or from other states?**

A huge amount is from out of state, but I get a lot of local people that call me, too. They'll e-mail me and say that they have seen my Website and can I help them find a piece of property. I will help them if it's a targeted area that I'm familiar with. If it's outside of the areas that I work and know well, then I'll refer them to someone else.

Q **I have found that to be true about every one of the high producers that I've talked to; they tend to work in a smaller area, but they know it intimately, and that's really important, I think.**

And you know what, Bob, actually you can know a few areas, but you can't know every area. When I first started in real estate, that was one of my biggest mistakes. I tried to get every little listing that I could get all over the place, but now I see that was a big mistake because I should have been concentrating on just a few areas that were closer and I could manage better.

Q *Do you ever do any telemarketing or cold calling of any sort?*

No, I don't.

Q *And Jessica doesn't either?*

No, we just don't do it.

Q *That's another theme that I've seen with all of the top performing agents that I have interviewed. What about mailings?*

Mailings! Yes, we do mailings three or four times a month, every month without fail.

Q *Same groups, same areas?*

Well, we kind of alternate. What Jessica does is to compile a list for me of various people to do target mailings to; in fact, what she did for me last year was to compile a list of doctors from all over town and we regularly send them marketing materials. I have made quite a number of sales from that activity.

What a great idea!

Q *Would you please describe for me what role your assistant plays in maintaining or increasing your effectiveness in these areas of getting business.*

Sure. There's the mailings. A lot of times, if I'm not there she can take calls. She knows the areas like I do and she can talk to people, set up appointments, send them information, direct them to my various Websites and tell them that this is where their property can be sold or they can find other properties to look at. Then there's the advertising; she handles all of that.

Q *She's licensed, right?*

Yes, she's licensed.

Q *What percent of your gross commission do you allocate in your business plan for marketing and advertising, and how do you track its effectiveness?*

I reserve at least 15 to 20 percent.

Q *That's right on the number with every other top performer that I've talked to.*

And how do I check its effectiveness? Well, the Websites really generate a lot of my business; I couldn't do without them. The most effective advertising that I have is *Homes & Land* magazine; it's just wonderful.

Q *When you decided to hire an assistant, did you set money aside to help pay for her until your sales increased?*

No, what I did was, I hired her part-time at first. I started her out part-time on an hourly basis at first.

Q *And then as your business grew, you just worked more hours into her schedule until she was full-time?*

That's right. It worked very well.

Q *Exactly when did you know that it was time to get an assistant?*

When I had paperwork piled up so high that I couldn't do anything else. I thought to myself, "I can't get another listing, I can't sell anything else, because I can't keep up with all of the paperwork." It was going to kill me. I couldn't keep up with the advertising. In fact, before I hired Jessica, I didn't do all of the advertising that I do now because there was no way that I could put all of the ads together by myself. That's when I decided, when the paperwork was higher than my head!

How did you find your assistant?

She is the daughter of a friend of mine that I've known for years. She had just graduated from high school and was going to Pima College. She was looking for a part-time job and the real estate company that I worked for then needed a part-time receptionist. She started there part time and eventually became the full-time receptionist. The agents went nuts over her because she was so organized and was very patient with everybody and that worked out great. Then she decided that she wanted to travel so she left the company and we didn't hear from her for a couple of years. Eventually she came back, and when she did, she looked me up and asked if there was anything that she can do, or did I need any help? She came right about the time that I decided that I needed some part-time help. She wasn't sure if she was going to stay in Tucson or go to school full-time, so I hired her temporarily and it has really worked out very well. I have actually known her since she was a little kid.

How many years have you guys been working together now?

We've been together for five years now.

Would you please describe the process that you used to interview Jessica, what you thought about before offering her the position, and how you hired her. I mean, you obviously knew her very well.

Yes, I did; you know, Bob, I really did. We went through a period of adjustment, of course, when she first started, mainly because I didn't know what I was doing, so it really wasn't her. She would take direction, but I didn't know how to direct her. We kind of learned how to work together. It would have been great to have some guidelines like you're doing here, but they weren't available then.

Q *One of the reasons that I'm writing this book is that I have found that so many people that I know who have assistants really struggled with them in the beginning because they really didn't know how to direct them to be effective assistants.*

We had problems because I didn't know what to tell her. If she did something wrong, it was usually my fault because I had told her to do it that way.

Q *Do you and Jessica meet regularly, and if so, how often do you meet?*

We consistently go out to lunch twice a week, and that's time away from the office and the phone. We have a nice lunch and we talk about things that we want to do and need to do. If she has suggestions, or she thinks that we need to be doing something, that's what we talk about. We do that every week, twice a week.

Q *That must give her a real sense of empowerment. Do you have a written agenda with you every time, or is it more informal?*

We both come with notes about what we want to talk about.

Q *What type of training, if any, did you give Jessica when you hired her?*

When I first hired her, it was on-the-job training. After a time, I paid for her to go to real estate school to get her license. Then a year later I sent her to school to learn how to create Websites, maintain them, and update them—the whole nine yards. It was a long training program and I paid for that.

Q *Interesting!*

So that has been a big savings for me and it's been wonderful for my business. She keeps the Websites current; she changes them and updates them for me all the time. My investment in her schooling has paid off big time!

Q *How do you think that has affected her feelings about herself and her abilities, to be that efficient?*

I think that it has given her a lot of self-esteem; I mean, you can see it, you can see how she's changed over the years.

Q *Do you have a written contract between you, and if so, would you briefly describe it to me?*

No, we really don't. The one thing that I don't have with her is a written contract.

Q *Have you created any forms or checklists that you and your assistant use for greater efficiency, and if you have, would you describe them for me, or better yet, will you give me a copy to use in the book?*

Sure, I'll give them to you. We have created forms and checklists. We have a checklist that we put in the file that Jessica uses; it's basically a rundown of everything that the people are supposed to sign, where the ads have been and all that. Every time that I advertise a property somewhere it is logged into that checklist, so that is really helpful.

Q *Have you worked your assistant into covering for you when you are on vacation and after hours?*

I have.

Q

How do you do that?

Well, we kind of alternate. I'm a phone call freak; I don't want to miss any calls. I say that I only work 40 hours a week, but I don't miss any calls at night or on weekends. So what we do is, basically one weekend a month she takes all of the calls. As far as vacations, she totally takes over when I'm gone. I don't go away for more than a couple of days at a time.

Q

When you're gone, do you check in or do you have any method of contacting her to see what's going on?

No, when I'm gone I put it completely in her hands. She knows where I'm at and if she needs something, she knows how to reach me. The last time that I went away, it was for three days. When I got back everything was just fine. The fact is that I really trust her.

Q

The nice thing about longevity is that you learn to really trust each other.

Yeah, I couldn't agree more!

Q

What programs or methods do you have in place to retain past clients and receive referrals from them?

I should probably do more. I do a mailing to all of them twice a year. I mail them a calendar at Christmas then I do another mailing in July. I stay in touch with my clients, pretty consistently anyway; you know, they become your friends. I get referrals from people that I knew ten years ago and that's nice. Other than that, I really don't do anything else.

Well, as busy as you are, it's obviously working very well for you.

Q

What does Jessica do for you to help you retain past clients and get new ones?

Well, she does the mailings, of course; I mean, she does them automatically.

Q *Do you have any input into the mailings or does she just do it?*

No, we talk about it each time. It's one of our common lunch topics. She'll say, "Here's the letter that I'm sending out," and I'll look it over and approve it first. What I didn't have before, that I have now with Jessica, is the TOP PRODUCER® program. She automatically enters everybody into it. If I had that five years ago I would have a phenomenal client base now. She enters their names, addresses, e-mail addresses, phone numbers and any other information that she has obtained.

Q *How many people are in your database?*

That's a good question. Let's see, at Christmas we sent out 800 calendars, so I've got a lot of people in there.

Yeah, that's good—that's quite a bit.

Q *How often do you contact the people in your database, and does it vary with the relationship that you have with them?*

I mail to the entire database twice a year, but there are a lot of people in there that I talk to every month, you know, people who have become good friends, people with real estate questions that stay in touch with me. Then there are people who see an ad in a real estate magazine and call me and say, "Oh, that's neat, where's that?" You know, that kind of stuff.

Q *Do you send them items of value on a regular basis to provide a service and keep in touch, and if you do, can you describe what you send to them? Also, please tell me what role your assistant plays in that activity.*

I don't. That's something that I really have planned to start doing this year. Actually, Jessica is after me all of the time to start doing something like that and asks me what I want to send them, so she's waiting for me to move a little faster. I'm getting comfortable with that idea.

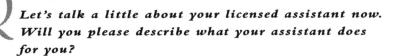

Let's talk a little about your licensed assistant now. Will you please describe what your assistant does for you?

Well, if I'm on appointments, I can be away from the office and she takes care of all of the calls and she tells people about the properties. I make sure that every time I list something that she goes and looks at it so that she has a firsthand knowledge of what she's talking about. She can quote prices to them, she can tell them about things that they want to know. She does all of the paperwork for every escrow that I open. When I get a listing, she goes and takes the pictures, she uploads them to the Websites, she gets the ads set up, and she does basically all of the paperwork so that I have free time to get more listings and talk to people. She does all of the behind-the-scenes work, but if I'm in the office and have the time, then I jump in and help her, too. But if I'm not there, I never have to worry about all of it getting done.

You don't list many houses, but when you do, does she go and put the keybox on, make the flyers and put them and the sign-in sheet at the property, that sort of thing?

Yes, and she routinely checks the flyer bins and keeps them full and puts new sign-in sheets in the homes, as necessary. With our electronic keysafe system, you can check on the MLS computer daily and see who has shown your listings, so she checks each of them daily and faxes each realtor a letter that asks them what they thought and what their client thought.

You know, if you call them, they will almost never call you back. I call people back because I want them to call me as well, so we found it was helpful to fax them a short three-line questionnaire that asks:

What did you think of the house?

Did your client like the house?

What do you think of the price?

Nine times out of ten we get an answer back. Then she sends those to the clients so that they know what the activity has been and what people have said about the property.

What hours and days of the week does your assistant work?

She's in the office Monday through Friday. I don't set hours for her but she tries to get there by 9:00 a.m. Sometimes she's there by 7:00, depending on what she has to accomplish that day, but she's always there by 9:00. She stays until everything is done, but she seldom leaves before 4:30 p.m.

What I'm trying to do with Jessica is to give her a sense of confidence that she's very capable of getting things done. She's not a secretary and I don't consider her to be one; she's an assistant and sets her own hours to get the job done and that makes her want to be there.

That makes perfect sense to me. Does she work weekends at all?

She will work weekends if I need her to. She'll do open houses if needed but I try to give her the weekends off so that she doesn't burn out. I don't stay in the office all day, every day. I think that people who stay in the office like that start to burn out after awhile. You know that.

That's so true!

How do you compensate Jessica?

Jessica gets a percentage of what I make, that's how she's paid.

Q *Around 10 percent, more or less?*

She was at 10 percent until this year. This year I raised it to 12 and a half percent.

Q *That's good. So she never worked on an hourly wage or anything, it's always been on a percentage basis?*

Well, when she first started with me, she worked hourly and that worked out okay for awhile, but then we had a hard time keeping track of her hours. Either she or I would forget to write down how many hours she worked and it got to be a pain, so we switched to a flat percentage of my earnings and it has worked out great!

Q *So it was just easier to pay her a flat percentage of what you make, when you make it?*

Yeah, we talked about it and I said to her, "You know how real estate is, one month you get a check and the next month you may not," but I didn't start the percentage thing until I had enough consistent business to make it all right for her. So that's when we went to the percentage and she's been happy with it. She knows it's a risk, but the more that I make, the more that she makes. That has motivated her to do more.

Q *Is your assistant an employee or an independent contractor, and why did you choose that method of employment?*

She's an independent contractor.

Q *So, basically she just gets a commission check from the company just like you do?*

Right, when I get paid, she gets paid.

Q *Would you talk to me about company support. How much office space do you and your assistant occupy?*

Well, we have a nice office; it's about 9 by 18 feet. We have two desks, a compter desk, and two doors, one that opens to a really nice patio with a floor to ceiling window. Then we have two file cabinets and a small refrigerator. I have a very good work space!

Q *What benefits does your company provide to you and your assistant? Any special advertising, accounting services for your assistant or anything like that?*

Well, let's see, they provide me my office, which is nice; they do't give me anything extra, but the office is nice and the staff is wonderful. That's another thing about Jessica, she interacts wonderfully with the staff.

Let's see, the company gives me "Longnet," the company intranet; it's an incredible tool. Then there is the company insert in the Sunday real estate section of the paper, the company real estate magazine, and things like that. They have a lot of stuff for everyone.

Q *In your opinion, is there anything that should be provided by the company that isn't being provided?*

No, they are even paying for a part of my mailings, which I though was nice, so I can't think of anything, unless they wanted to pay for Jessica.

Q *Yeah, that would be nice. Let's talk for a few minutes; I want to get your opinion on some things. Producing the very high sales volume that you have done every year for so many years clearly sets you apart from the average real estate agent. What do you do that's so different from them?*

I think all of my consistent marketing helps me a lot.

Q *And that's pretty focused to the same group most of the time?*

It really is. It's that and the other mailings. I think that most agents are way too inconsistent with their mailings. They'll do a few and if they don't get a response they'll quit, probably right before it was starting to make an impact.

I also make sure that if I do a transaction with another realtor, I want them to walk away saying, "Yeah, I'm glad that I worked with Debbie." I make sure that they are not going to have a bad experience with me. Sometimes they're such a knucklehead that you can't help it, but you know that right away, and you probably aren't going to see them again anyway.

Q *Yeah, they're the kind that seem to come and go.*

They sure are!

Q *What role does Jessica play in the activities that make you so effective, such as the mailings and other things?*

Actually, I don't do the mailings; she does all of them. She does everything. I just look over some things before she sends them out. She really does all of the "back-room" stuff for me.

Q *In your opinion, what is the single biggest benefit that you bring to your clients?*

I would have to say, experience and specialization learned over many years, and staying in the marketplace. I made a choice to specialize in land and I really know what I'm doing in that arena. I am called on to do home sales often enough that I stay well-informed about that market as well and I research everything very carefully, so there's no guesswork in what I do.

> **Q**
>
> *So, you benefit clients by being very aware of the market and being very up-to-date on your marketing tools and information?*

That's exactly right. I mean, the rules and regulations change all the time, too. I make sure that I stay on top of all that.

> **Q**
>
> *How is your ability to deliver this benefit to your clients enhanced by your assistant?*

Well, for example, Jessica is always looking for real-estate-related articles, online and in the newspapers and magazines. When she sees one she always brings it to me, then' of course, she does the complete mailings for me without my even saying anything. Every time that I list or sell something, she automatically does a *just listed* or *just sold* mailing for me. We use our own postcards for that, we don't use the company ones.

> **Q**
>
> *Tell me where you see the real estate agent's role in the home or land buying process going in the next several years, and how you see that role enhanced by the use of a licensed assistant.*

I think that people will continue to want more personal contact about their particular listing, and they will expect more consistent contact. They will want almost constant contact instead of every so often, and I think that the assistant is the perfect person to give that added dimension of client contact that people are looking for while the agent is out looking for more business. People know a lot more about real estate today than they used to and they have a higher expectation of us; rightly so, I think.

> **Q**
>
> *I think that the Internet and the "Home Show" related television programs have made for a much better-educated consumer, and I think that's great!*

I really agree. I like it when I'm dealing with a savvy consumer.

Q *People seem to come to us now, and they're very savvy and they pretty much know what they want and it saves us a lot of time trying to find out what it is that they are trying to achieve.*

Yeah, I agree with you 100 percent.

Q *What are the top three pieces of advice that you can give to a real estate agent who is thinking about hiring a licensed assistant?*

I would say, to make sure that you are going to get along with this person. Investigate their background and check them out carefully.

If I hired someone new now, I would hire them on a trial basis for at least a couple of months to be sure that they are what I really want. It is often not easy to deal with other agents and you've gotta have someone who's not overly sensitive and doesn't take things personally, because people can sometimes be mean.

Lastly, if you're doing any kind of volume sales at all, I just can't imagine trying to do business without an assistant today. I could do a lot more business than I'm doing now, but I'm enjoying my family life and I'm doing what I want to do and I'm making exactly what I want to make, so how much better can it get?

Q *It's all a matter of choice. We have a mutual acquaintance who has built a large team and I don't see that person being any happier than you, or even as happy as you have been over the years.*

Well, I'll tell you what I'm doing; I'm consistent and I'm in it for the long run and I don't want to get so big that it isn't fun for me anymore. I'd like to do this for the next 25 years and Jessica has helped me to achieve that consistency.

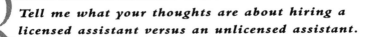

Q *Tell me what your thoughts are about hiring a licensed assistant versus an unlicensed assistant.*

I think that you have to have a licensed assistant. I think that an unlicensed assistant is a secretary, that's what I think. They can do all the paperwork for you, and that's about it. A licensed assistant can go out for you to put on or remove a keybox, check the property inside if it's vacant, open a house up for someone, meet people at a property for you and a whole lot more, but they must be licensed.

Q *A bigger bang for the buck.*

Absolutely! And I think that it's worth paying to get someone licensed if you have confidence in them. If you pay to have that training done for someone it repays you over and over again. Like the Website school that I sent Jessica to that has repaid me over and over again many times.

Q *Is there anything else that you would like to tell the person who is reading this book?*

Yes. Definitely don't treat an assistant like a secretary. I mean, have confidence that they can do things and don't micromanage them; that's the worst thing that you can do. Giving them flexibility and responsibility builds their self-confidence as they are working with you.

Another thing is to go with their strengths. Whatever it is that they really excel at, just let them do it and reap the rewards; conversely, if they are uncomfortable with something, don't make them do it over and over until they hate it. Stay with their strengths.

Debbie, that's great advice. Thank you very much.

Conversations with Two Licensed Assistants

*I*nterview with Eileen Herd, REPA—
Roy Long Realty Co.
Oro Valley, Arizona

Bob Herd's comments are in bold and italicized type.
Eileen Herd's comments are in regular type.

Q

Eileen, tell the readers a little about what you did prior to your real estate career.

We have four children, so after working as an executive secretary for a major bank for several years I decided to be a stay-at-home mom and raise our children until they were out of school. I felt that it was important.

Q

When did you start a career in real estate?

Well, I got my California license in 1976. With your being in real estate I thought that it would be a good idea for me to have one as well, just in case you needed any backup or anything. I got my Arizona license when we moved to Scottsdale in 2000.

Q

Do you have any professional designations from the National Association of REALTORS®, and if you do, why do you think that's important?

Yes, after I got my real estate license here in Arizona, I made a decision that I wanted to work in a support role and not as an agent, so I took the Real Estate Professional Assistant's course and got the REPA designation. I think that it's a very good designation to get.

Even though I had a long tenure in real estate sales with you in California and worked as your backup person on many occasions, the course really put it all together for me as to how to really be an excellent assistant; it's a very good course to take if you're planning on becoming an assistant, and you should put the designation on your business card.

Q *Why do you think it's important and how does it help you to become a better assistant?*

Well, for someone new to the real estate business, it gives you a fabulous overview of the business and what your role in the process is. Even if you are very experienced, like me, it just gives you added knowledge of the home buying and selling process from start to finish, including the entire escrow process. It also details what type of things can be done to support a very busy agent; I couldn't recommend it more highly.

Q *Did you start as an agent first, or did you start in a support position?*

I started pretty much in a support position in your company when you owned it, and then I became an agent after you sold it. We have worked together several times over the years with me either in sales when you were in management, or in a support position with you when you were in sales.

Q *Tell me about the positions that you have had since we moved to Arizona.*

I have been strictly in a support position since we moved here. It's been interesting and very gratifying.

Q

What did you like the best about it?

The fast-paced environment. I've handled as many as 27 open escrows at a time, with 20-something being the norm and the phone calls are constant. The sheer challenge of it makes for a great job. It can be stressful at times, though.

Q

You've worked for some pretty high-powered sales executives. Could you please tell us a little bit about them—what their annual sales volume was and how many units they did.

Well, the first agent that I worked for here in Arizona did around $15 million in sales volume a year. The next one that I worked for started around $10 to $12 million a year, and after I came on board and was able to help her, she did over $40 million in volume last year.

Q

You were very instrumental in helping her to increase her volume, weren't you?

Yes, I loved that job and really went all out to help her in every way that I could.

Q

What are some of the differences in how those two operate and how they worked with you as an assistant?

The first gal that I worked with did a lot of upscale home sales. She listed a $15 million property when I was working for her. She also had a lot of contractor clients and she listed a lot of custom-built homes.

Q

And that was in Scottsdale, right?

Yes, that was in Scottsdale.

Q   *What's the difference between how she worked and how the second agent that you worked for operated?*

The second gal pretty much started off in a partnership with another lady that primarily did land transactions and knew land sales very well. When they started, they had two or three subdivisions listed. They were pretty big, averaging 70-plus lots each. They sold them out.

Her husband was a contractor as well, so she learned a lot about custom home construction and sales. She did a lot of self-promoting and ended up working with a lot of contractors and did a lot of custom home sales. The other contractors never seemed to have an issue with her husband's being a contractor as well because she did such a great job for all of them.

Q   *About how many escrows a month did you have going on, in an average month?*

On average, I had between 15 and 25, all the time.

Q   *Let's talk about you and about your job description. Are you strictly in the office or are you in and out?*

I was very seldom out of the office. With everything that was going on, and given that I handled all of the details for every escrow and input and maintained all of the listings, I had very little time available to get out of the office. I used to work right through lunch most of the time, although I don't recommend that. A person needs a break during the day to regroup. I would eat while I worked. I would go and open up a house once in awhile, but that was the exception, not the rule. As busy as the agent was that I worked for, I multitasked constantly.

Q   *Both of the agents that you worked for carried a very large listing inventory, too, isn't that correct?*

That's right.

Q

Did you get a lot of calls on those listings?

I sure did. It was my job to field all of those calls and disburse them to the agent or the buyer's reps, as directed and necessary. I made a *lot* of money for everyone on the team by the way that I handled those calls.

Q

Would you please describe what your duties are, and how they have varied from agent to agent.

Okay. The first gal that I worked for, I usually prepared all of the listing paperwork and I handled all of her escrows. At times I would even be available to hold an open house on a Sunday or for the REAL-TORS® tour. When I started working for the other gal, I did everything. I did all of the advertising; I would input and maintain all of the listings and I handled all of the escrows from start to finish. That was when she was at about $12 to $15 million volume. As she grew, it became impossible for one person to do all of that so, after the first year she started adding buyer's reps and other support people to the team to keep up with everything.

Q

Did you make property brochures and do mail outs?

I did at first. I used consistently to do the mail outs, the "just listed" and "just sold" cards, and make the property brochures and I used to send letters into certain subdivisions to get new listings. As we grew, I was too busy to do that any longer.

Q

How have you and the agents that you have worked for handled weekend and vacation coverage?

I would take about a week off every year, and that would be preplanned with the agent. I used to field weekend calls when the agent was away and either handled the issue myself or referred the caller to another team member, as was appropriate. All of her calls came to me as a sort of "clearing house," and then I would decide how to best handle it.

Regarding vacations, the agent in Scottsdale had another agent in the office handle all of her buyers and buyer calls; I handled everything else. The other agent would have me take all of her calls when she was away, and then make a determination as to how to best handle each one. That was very efficient.

Q

Have you created any forms that have made your job or the agent's job easier or more productive or efficient, and if you have, would you please describe them to us?

The larger companies all have their own forms for controlling listing and sales files, so I pretty much just used their forms. I also had a communications log that I maintained and turned in when each escrow closed, but I didn't create any special forms. We had some forms that were specific to the team that we all developed to suit our special needs, mostly about transitioning from a listing file to a sales file.

Q

Did you find that the company forms were adequate to maintain your files?

Yes, they were just fine and we never had a problem, but we also used the team-specific forms as well and that made the job even easier for everyone.

Q

Do you do anything to help the agent retain past clients and obtain referrals from them?

If it was a listing, then there has already been contact with me on several occasions; if it is a new contract where we have the buyer, then I start and maintain the contact throughout the escrow. I try to really get to know clients on a personal basis and treat them right. I stay in constant touch and quickly get answers to all of their questions. After the escrow closes, I get the closing gift for the agent and get the keys from the client and handle any after-closing issues that come up. Then I put them on our mailing list and they receive something in the mail from us every month.

Q

About how many people are in the agent's database?

Probably about 600 or so.

Q

Does she do any type of regular communication with them, and if so, what does she do, and what is your role in the process?

She mails out once a month, and she stays in touch by sending them timely information about real estate matters in general. From time to time she sends them comparable sales in their subdivision. She gets a lot of referrals that way. She does a lot of mailing and after we grew to a certain point, it was too much for me to handle so she has another team member do this function.

Q

With her sales volume growing past the $40 million mark the last year that you worked for her, she really had to expand her team in order to keep up with everything, right?

That's right. I ended up working over 50 hours a week on a regular basis and I had gone past my ability to do it all, so she needed to add staff just to keep the operation moving along in an orderly fashion.

Q

Let's talk about the hiring process. Please describe the process that was used when you were hired.

Well, the first agent that I worked for responded to a letter that I sent out to all of the branch managers of the major companies and a group of people in the real estate association that were known top agents. This lady had just lost her assistant and was looking for a replacement. She called me and we met. She called me back later that day and asked if I would like to start work the following day.

As you know, the second agent was an introduction from you when you were her branch manager. We clicked right away, and since you had told her so much about me, she hired me on the spot. That was a nice feeling and the start of a great relationship; I really enjoyed working for her.

Q

Did either of them ask you to fill out any type of preemployment form?

No, the only thing that I was asked to do was to fill out the standard company hire form.

Q

Did the agents have a list of questions that they asked you, or was the interview sort of off-the-cuff?

It was pretty much off-the-cuff.

Q

Were you offered the job right away, or did they wait and call you later?

In both cases I was offered the job right away or the same day.

Q

Were you given the position for a probationary period of time, or did they just offer you the job?

We never discussed it; I was just hired.

Q

Were you given a contract to sign, and if not, has this ever caused any problems between you?

No, I was never asked to sign a contract. The only problem that I encountered was that when you got the manager's position in Tucson and we moved, the agent was really upset and said that I had to give her six weeks' notice. I said that I couldn't do that and she was very put out, to say the least.

The second agent that I worked for just jotted the basics down on a piece of paper for me and that was it; neither of us ever signed anything.

Q **You worked for her for about three and a half years, right?**

Yes, that's right; and during the last part of my tenure with her, she was restructuring her team and drastically reduced my bonuses. I was there from the beginning and really expected a discussion before having my compensation changed.

Q **I remember that. Could you have been better protected by having a written contract?**

By all means; I am specific about requesting a written contract now. I used to work a lot of extra hours that I didn't get paid for on an hourly wage, but the bonus made it worthwhile. When that went away it just wasn't worth it.

Q **Did you start full-time right away or did you start part-time and increase your hours as the agent's business grew?**

With the first lady in Scottsdale, it was part-time at first for a very short time. Then after she saw the value of what I brought to the table and how much it freed her up to generate more business, it quickly became a full-time position. The second position was full-time right away.

Yeah, she was in dire need of someone full time right away. I still remember calling her into my office and telling her to get an assistant before she got ill from all of the work.

Q **Tell us how your salary was negotiated and how you got paid.**

Well, I was very experienced and required a minimal amount of training. I was very escrow savvy. I merited a top-scale salary. I had to make the first agent aware of what she was getting before she understood that I was worth more than the minimum, but the second agent offered me a very generous top-scale hourly wage and bonus right away. I earned every dollar and never let either of them down. I really helped them to grow their businesses, too.

Q

All right, let's talk about the training process now. Were you given any training as to how to do the job, either by the agent or by the company that they worked for, and if you were, would you please describe how you were trained?

In both cases there were some classes that the company made me go through; everyone new to the company had to. Other than that, I was not formally trained by anyone. The training took place as a sort of running dialogue with the agent. Some sort of job description would have been a great help.

Q

Of course you picked it up quickly because of your many years as an agent and from being my assistant for many years.

And, of course, I had never sold land before, but when you and the agent that you work for are doing large subdivisions, you really pick it up fast. I really learned subdivisions; all about public reports, surveys, site-grading issues, percolation tests and everything else. Of course, if you are buying or selling raw, unsubdivided land, then there are many more issues as well.

Q

Were you computer–literate when you were hired, and if not, what was done to get you trained?

To a degree. I could handle the MLS computer system, do word processing, and keep a database updated, but I'm not a whiz by any means. I was self-taught as I went along and learned things that were important to the agent's business. No one ever sat down with me and said, "Here, I'm going to teach you how to access the County Assessor's database," or anything like that. I'm self-taught.

Q

Let's talk about how you, as a licensed assistant, work effectively with an agent. What have the agents that you have worked for done to empower you and make you feel like a part of their team?

When they introduced me to their clients, and when they would take me along with them on a listing presentation and introduce me as their assistant, they would explain to the client that I handled all of the paperwork and that when the property sold, I would be handling all of the escrow issues as well. Each client understood that we would be really full service through the entire listing and sale process and beyond. Really stressing this to each client was the source of many referrals.

Q

Did any of them ever take the time to tell you that you were doing a great job or congratulate you, or anything of that nature?

Yes, they all did. They were very good about that; it made me feel very good.

Q

What have any of them done in the past to alienate you and maybe even make you decide to leave their employ?

That's a little bit tough. Pretty much a change in their attitude. It seems that they can sometimes get so caught up in their success that they forget who helped them to achieve much of it. They start to take you for granted. With one of them, everyone in the office saw how much time I was putting in. Most nights I was the last one out of the office. I didn't mind doing it, even if it was after-hours and I wasn't getting paid for it, because I enjoyed the job, but it got to where it just didn't matter to her. That's when the job became unpleasant.

Q

So you feel that the agent's taking the time to recognize you for the work that's done by you as an assistant is an important thing?

I think that's very true, because if you go ahead and appreciate both a job well done and the time that a person puts in that's over and above what they need to do, you've got to take the time to consider that they are helping you build your business faster and better than you could do it alone.

Q

Was there ever a time when your role as the assistant was not clearly defined by the agent, and if so, what kind of problems did that create?

Yes! Although I am perfectly willing to assist with a showing appointment once in awhile, I never did want to be a buyer's representative. One agent that I worked for thought that being her assistant meant that I was to show property for her on demand at any time, even the weekends, and she wasn't even willing to pay me a referral fee if I sold them something.

She would go out of town one weekend a month and expected me to fully step in for her without even asking me at the interview and with no extra compensation except for an hourly wage; that was totally unrealistic. It turned out that she really didn't have enough work for me anyway and we didn't last long. I have never minded working late during the week, but if I wanted to work seven days a week I would go back to being an agent without an assistant.

Q

What kind of problems did that create?

Plenty; she should have made it very clear at the interview that she was looking for someone to step in as a substitute agent much of the time. She never told me that she expected anything more than escrow and listing maintenance and an occasional showing, but it sure turned out to be something different. It ended up being a very short-term relationship.

Q

How often do you meet with the agent that you work for now, and how is that different from the previous agent that you worked for?

The previous agent that I worked for had built a team of several people and we used to have a team meeting every Wednesday morning at 8:30 a.m. I used to come to the meeting with all of the open escrows printed out and a list of all of the current listings. My job was to go over them one by one so that everyone on the team had an up-to-date analysis of what was going on. The agent and I would meet informally a couple of times a week as well.

The agent that had the large team obviously had much higher expenses, with payroll and all. Did you meet regularly to review the escrow closings to analyze her cash flow position?

Absolutely. I used to keep track of all of the escrow closings and the amount of commission that was coming to her, for exactly that purpose.

On average, how many hours a week do you work now, and how is that different from other agents that you have worked for?

Right now I work 40 hours a week, often with a few extra, as needed. I used to work between 55 to 60 hours when I was on the big team.

Have any of the agents that you have worked for ever asked you to help them to create an annual business plan, and if so, what input could you give that was helpful?

They all had their own personal advisor or CPA and they would do their own planning. All of them would ask my opinion about operational things throughout the year though.

Are you now, or have you ever been, an employee, or have you always been an independent contractor?

I've worked as an employee. The company would do the payroll and the deductions and they would charge the agent my salary plus 10.1 percent to handle all of it. I was technically an employee of the company, but I worked on an at-will contract with the agent.

Q *In your opinion, what's the single biggest benefit that you bring to the agent that you work for?*

By being very savvy about the sale and escrow process I always know just how to handle most any situation that arises. I can take care of issues that come up in a proper way that keeps everyone happy with minimal or no input from the agent. My people skills are also a great help in making the home buying or selling process a very pleasant one for the clients and that helps the agent to maintain clients and receive referrals from them.

One of the agents that I worked for was very high-strung. She constantly said that I was a leveling influence on her and helped to keep her grounded.

Q *Eileen, what are the top three pieces of advice that you could give to a person who wants to work as a licensed assistant?*

Well, let's see. First and foremost, learn your craft well. Really get to know the listing and sales contract in your area very, very well. It's amazing how much power and control that gives you when you are dealing with people in a real estate transaction.

Stay calm and treat everyone fairly, whether it's a client, a builder, or another agent. The fact is that you *are* going to work with that person more than once and if you maintained a professional attitude in your prior encounters with them it will be of great benefit to you over and over.

The third thing is to stay very current in your knowledge of the marketplace and the real estate business in general. This business changes constantly and the more you stay informed, the more valuable you are to the agent that you work for and to the clients.

> ### Do you think that there is value in an agent's working with an unlicensed assistant?

Well, the value of an unlicensed assistant to the agent is minimal. Unlicensed assistants can only give minimal information over the telephone; they can't put keyboxes on or take them off, they can't field telephone inquiries about properties that the agent has listed, they can't open a home for the agent. There is just so little that they can really do without crossing the line and getting both themselves and the agent that they work for in trouble because they are practicing real estate without a license. The other issue is the standard of care that comes with the knowledge that is obtained by getting a license. As an assistant, you're so much better prepared to handle the job the right way with a license.

> ### Would you advise the agents and the assistants to have a written contract between them?

Yes, I would. I think that it's really important to set forth the requirements and expectations of each party.

> ### Is there anything else that you would like to tell the person who is reading this book?

If you like working in the real estate industry, but you want your weekends free, or you are raising a family and you want hours that are more defined, then working as a licensed assistant is really the way to go. It's exciting being somewhat the power behind the throne. The job is quite gratifying and pays very well.

Interview with Jessica Phillips—
Roy Long Realty Co.
Tucson, Arizona

Bob Herd's comments are in bold and italicized type.
Jessica Phillips' comments are in regular type.

Jessica, let's start with a little about your background. What did you do prior to your real estate career?

I started working as a receptionist with Tucson Realty & Trust Co. They promoted me into one of the administrative positions. I did that for a couple of years.

So you had some time around the real estate industry prior to becoming an assistant?

Yes; I did take a break for about two years, and then I came back into it.

Do you feel that the time that you spent in the administrative position helped you in your career as a licensed assistant?

Yes, I do believe that it helped me a lot because I was already familiar with the paperwork and forms when I started. I knew what to look for in the way of signatures and forms; I was just that much sharper.

When did you start your career as a licensed assistant?

August of 2000.

Q

Have you ever been licensed in another state?

No.

Q

Do you hold any professional designations from the National Association of Realtors®?

Not at this time.

Q

They have a designation called the Real Estate Professional Assistant (REPA). Have you ever considered taking that class?

I have considered it. I haven't done it yet, but I will be taking it in the near future.

Q

So you didn't start as an agent first; you started in an administrative position first and then went right into a licensed assistant's position, is that correct?

Yes.

Q

You have worked for Debbie Green ever since you started, isn't that right?

Yes, I've known Debbie for many years prior to going into real estate and have worked with her ever since I started as an assistant.

Q

Would you please tell us a little about her, that is, her annual sales volume and the average number of transactions that she does.

She does about $10 to $15 million in volume every year and anywhere from 50 to 110 transactions a year.

Q ***And she does primarily land sales, isn't that right?***

Yes.

Q ***She does houses by referral and repeat business only, is that right?***

Yes.

Q ***Tell me about your job description. Are you strictly in the office or are you in and out?***

I'm in the office about 75 percent of the time and out in the field about 25 percent of the time. It depends on what is needed; I'll do open houses, show property, or whatever she needs me to do.

Q ***Would you please describe your duties and how they have varied since you started?***

Well, Debbie does a lot of listings, so I routinely set up the listing. I verify all of the property information, I make sure that the for sale sign is ordered if one is needed, I take digital pictures of the property, and I make listing packages and property brochures and constantly keep them updated in the event of any changes. I do mailings, I write all of the advertising, I designed our Website and keep it current, and anything else that comes up that she needs me to do.

Q ***That's pretty impressive! I understand that she paid for you to go to school to learn to build and maintain Websites?***

Yes, she did.

Q ***How much of an asset do you think that has been?***

Oh, I think that it's been a large asset to her because she doesn't have to pay another company just to design her Website and continually update it; I can do it much more quickly than an outside vendor can do it, so it's much more responsive to her business needs.

Other things that I do are to keep tabs on the listing and escrow paperwork and see that it all gets signed and delivered and turned in to the company on time. We have all of our listings in a book along with plat maps and other pertinent information that we fax out to people who call in. I keep all of that current so that when an agent or a buyer calls and wants information on one of our listings, they get it immediately and it's always up to date. I also mail out all of the ads to the clients so that they can see what we are doing for them.

Q

That's very comprehensive! How do you and Debbie schedule your vacations and weekend coverage?

Well, we are just in the process of my taking all of her calls one complete weekend a month, but we haven't started yet. Regarding vacations, I just take all of the calls and if there's something really important that I know needs her attention then I can call her, but for the most part I try not to. I haven't had to do that yet, so we're very well covered as far as that goes.

Q

Have you created any programs or forms that make your job or Debbie's job easier or more productive? If you have, would you please describe them to us?

Well, the book that we have in the office is a major asset. We are always looking for the book as it has everything in it that we need. Debbie usually has over 50 active listings at any given time, so having all of the information on them close at hand and in a very orderly fashion is a real plus and makes our work easier and more productive. We get a huge amount of business from the Website. Other than that, we just use the company forms.

Q

Do you do anything to help Debbie retain past clients and receive referrals from them?

We use the TOP PRODUCER® computer program and we constantly do mailings. We send out calendars to Debbie's entire client base every year and then we do two types of mailings; one is a periodic mailing to her client base, just to keep in touch, and the other ones are spot mailings that I do to areas where there are tracts of land in population growth areas. That is obvious potential business for Debbie. I do the spot mailings on my own and just tell Debbie where I have sent a mailing to, so if she gets a call she will know the source.

About how many people are in Debbie's database?

I don't have an exact number, but it's quite a few because she has been in business for a long time.

Does she do any type of regular communication with the people in her database, and if so, what does she do and what is your role in it?

Well, we are in constant communication with the owners of the properties that we have listed. We send them copies of ads and information about showings and client or agent feedback. Postcards go out in areas where we have properties listed, just updating the neighbors about what is happening in their area and, of course, I do the spot mailings to what I think are potential growth areas where land is going to be sold. I do all of this myself as a regular part of my job and I keep Debbie informed about what I have done.

Let's talk about the hiring process. Please describe the process that was used when you were hired by Debbie.

I actually called her and she and her partner were looking for someone to work for them. When they first started out they just needed someone to do a little paperwork and mailings. At that time they were a new partnership and they weren't sure about what they needed; they were just sort of thrown into it. There really wasn't any definition to the job and I just started doing what needed the most attention at the time.

Q *Were you asked to fill out any type of preemployment form?*

No, I wasn't.

Q *Because of the prior relationship with Debbie?*

That's right.

Q *Did Debbie or her partner have a list of questions that they asked you, to determine your capabilities, or was the interview sort of off-the-cuff?*

No, it was very informal because she knew that I had the past experience with the real estate company in a support role, so that did help a lot.

Q *Did they offer you the job right away or did they think about it and call you back?*

No, we agreed right then.

Q *So it was more informal?*

That's right.

Q *Were you hired for a probationary period, or did they just offer you the job?*

I started out part time. I would come to the office in the evenings or come in during the week and just do whatever they threw at me to do. They didn't need me for about six months and then I came back full-time. They had some transitional things going on and it was just too much for me, so after that cleared up I came back full time, but technically I was never in a probationary period.

Q

Were you given any kind of a contract to sign, and if not, did this ever cause any problems between you?

No, I've never signed a contract and it has never been a problem.

Q

Tell us how and when your salary was negotiated and how you are paid.

At first, I wasn't full time so I was paid hourly. No negotiations really took place; they just said to me, "if you want the job, this is what you'll get paid," and it just went from there. That's all the negotiating there was.

Q

What was your hourly wage when you worked part time?

When I first started with them I was unlicensed and they paid me ten dollars an hour. After I got licensed it changed. The partnership had ended and I was just working for Debbie, so instead of an hourly wage, I got a percentage of each of her commissions.

Q

So you get paid a straight commission every time Debbie closes an escrow. It's about 12 percent of what she gets, if I'm not mistaken.

That's right.

Q

Now, let's talk about the training process. Were you given any training as to how to do the job, either by Debbie or by the company that she worked for, and if you were, would you please describe how you were trained?

No, actually I wasn't. I wasn't trained by the company at all. Debbie paid for me to get my real estate license and she paid for me to go to school to learn how to design and maintain Websites, but I never had any formal training; I just learned as I went along by doing the job.

Q

Were you computer literate when you were hired, and if not, what was done to get you trained and what have you learned since?

Yes, I'm computer literate and I think that's one of the things that has really helped us because I'm really quick with it and I can make it work to our advantage; it's a great tool.

Q

Debbie is primarily into land and subdivision sales. Does that require any specialized knowledge on your part in order to be more effective at your job?

Yes, it really does. The type of information that I need to verify to give proper disclosures is much different from that needed in home sales. I have to have a very good understanding of zoning issues, knowledge of master plan issues, legal versus physical access, location and availability of utilities and those kinds of issues.

If I was doing strictly residential sales, then I wouldn't need that type of knowledge, but I sure do need it for what we do.

Q

Did Debbie train you on the specialized knowledge that you needed?

Not formally; it was more by example. Whenever she would get into something that I hadn't already learned, she would always take the time to explain to me what she was doing and why. I made it a point to always listen carefully to what she was doing, but I never had any formal "sit-down" training from her.

Q

Do you feel that the Real Estate Professional Assistant (REPA) designation that the National Association of REALTORS® offers is worth obtaining, and if you do, why do you think so?

I do. I've learned about some of the things that are taught in that course and it is something that I feel will enhance my abilities as an assistant. I'll be taking it soon.

Q

Let's talk about working effectively with an agent. What has Debbie done to empower you and make you feel like a part of her team?

She increasingly gives me more responsibilities and she treats me like a peer. I mean, I know what to do and she doesn't sit there and tell me how to do my job and micromanage me to death. She just lets me do my job. I have my own schedule and I do what I need to do every day to get the day's work done. She trusts me to do that and that is something that makes me feel like an important part of her team.

Q

She treats you more like a partner than an employee, so to speak.

Exactly!

Q

Has she, or her partner, when she had one, ever done anything to alienate you and almost make you want to leave her employ?

She never has, but at the time when she was in the partnership there were times when it got ugly with the partner and there was a time when I was ready to leave. I sat down with her and I told her that I couldn't do this anymore. There was a very high stress level going on between them and everyone was feeling it. The other agent was very condescending to me and I got to a point where I couldn't tolerate it any longer. The partnership broke up shortly after that.

Q

Was there ever a time when your role as an assistant was not clearly defined by Debbie, and if so, what kind of problems did that create?

You know, I'm sure that there were times, but I can't recall any specific instances right now. We have such good communication between us that every time a situation like that comes up, we just talk through it and move on.

Q *Those situations usually occur when new things come in to play that the agent hears about and doesn't convey to you, and then you do business as usual and it's not the right thing. In my interview with Debbie it became very clear that the two of you have excellent communication between you; you meet regularly for lunch and bring notes and go over issues and that sort of thing.*

Yeah, and if either of us sees or hears of something new, we always make sure that the other person knows about it, too. It's just good business.

Q *Debbie told me that you are constantly on the look-out for new ideas and business-related articles through the Internet and the papers and when you find them, you bring them in and see that she gets them. She said that she really appreciates that.*

Yes, I do that. If I see something that's in an area that we are working in or just anything that will keep us both up to date on what we do, I always bring it to her attention.

Q *How often do you meet with Debbie? Where do you meet? What do you discuss, and do you have an agenda?*

We don't have a formal agenda but we often bring notes. We meet every Tuesday and Thursday for lunch and we just talk about different work things that are going on. When she is in the office, we frequently discuss different things that are happening, like the various transactions and those types of things. We bring notes to our meetings if we have any really important or detailed topics to go over.

Q *On average, how many hours a week do you work now, and how is that different from when you first started?*

It all depends on how busy it is. From Monday through Friday it could be from 40 to 45 or 50 hours, depending on how crazy it is. At other times, like in the summer, we're not in as often. We try to take Tuesdays and Thursdays off and work the rest of the week. Monday, Wednesday, and Friday we are in the office and we play the weekends by ear. We've done that the last two summers and it has worked really well. We both have home offices, so the other days we just work from home.

What an interesting concept!

Has Debbie ever asked you to help her create an annual business plan, and if so, what input did you give that was helpful?

We will sit down and discuss ad budgets for the coming year, but we have never done an annual budget together. We do make goals for ourselves at the beginning of each year, so I guess that's kind of an informal business plan.

That's true. In addition to that, it seems to me that you help her to stay very focused all year long by some of the things that you do.

We each have our own things that we do, but I don't just wait for her to give me things to do. I go on my own a lot of the time and I'll tell her, "Hey, I'm doing this mailing to this area," and she'll just say "Okay." I keep busy constantly with things that seem to make sense to create more business or keep the current clients happy. As long as we keep putting the energy into the business, it always seems to come back to us.

Have you ever worked as an employee, or have you always been an independent contractor?

I was considered an employee when I was part-time and unlicensed, but I have been an independent contractor ever since I became full-time and licensed.

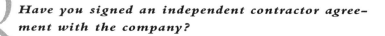

Q *Have you signed an independent contractor agreement with the company?*

Yes.

Q *In your opinion, what is the single biggest benefit that you bring to Debbie's operation, and how does it make her more effective?*

I think by doing all of the paperwork and tying up loose ends, she can go out and be in the field and list and sell more property, which I think is a really big bonus. I pick up her calls when she is out in the field. The people who call seem to really like getting a real live person instead of a recording and I can very often resolve things right on the spot for her.

Q *She mentioned that to me as well, so basically, you keep her right on the cutting edge all the time?*

That's right.

Q *What are the top three pieces of advice that you can give to someone who wants to work as a licensed assistant?*

To be flexible. I think that you can't be too one-dimensional; you have to be able to switch your gears all the time. I mean, the phone call that you pick up while you're doing your paperwork is often going to change your day, so don't get fixated on any one thing and just take it as it comes.

Learn the product well. You have to know the agent that you work for and what he or she is working with. Take the time to visit his or her listings and get firsthand knowledge about them so that you can tell people about them. Get to know the buyers as well so that you can be on the lookout for property for the agent to show them.

My third piece of advice is continuing education. Keep yourself updated on all of the changes in the rules, regulations, and forms that are constantly taking place and have a current understanding of what is going on in the real estate market.

Jessica, is there anything else that you would like to tell the person who is reading this book?

Well, I think that the stress level of the real estate industry can sometimes be a little overwhelming, so keep yourself focused and never stray from the things in your life that are important to you. Essentially, learn to live with it, but don't let it turn your whole world upside down.

Appendices: Sample Employment Forms and Checklists from Mega-Producers

Appendix A

Licensed Assistant
Preemployment Application

Full name _____

Address _____

City, State, Zip _____

Telephone numbers: Home _____Cell _____

E-mail address _____

DOB **(D/M ONLY)** _____

Driver's license # _____

Soc. Security # _____

(You will be required to present both if you are offered employment.)

How far do you live from this location? _____

Do you have your own transportation? _____

EMPLOYMENT HISTORY
(Start with most recent)

Employer name/phone   From   To

_____

Duties:

_____
_____
_____
_____

Preemployment Application, continued

Employer name/phone   From   To

_____

Duties:

_____

_____

_____

_____

Employer name/phone   From   To

_____

Duties:

_____

_____

_____

_____

By initialing below, you are giving us permission to contact your previous employers.

_____

Initial here

PERSONAL REFERENCES:

Name _____

Address _____

Telephone number _____

Relationship _____

Years known _____

Name _____

Address _____

Telephone number _____

Relationship _____

Years known _____

Name _____

Address _____

Telephone number _____

Relationship _____

Years known _____

By initialing below, you are giving us permission to contact your references.

_____

Initial here

Licensed Assistant
Interview Sheet

1. Are you currently licensed in this state? If yes, for how long?

2. Are you licensed in any other state? If so, do you plan to return there?

3. Tell me about your real estate career if you've had one, and why you decided on a real estate career.

4. Are you currently employed? If so, where and for how long?

5. Why are you making the transition from sales to a licensed assistant position?

6. What is the best job that you've ever had and what did you like the most about it?

7. What former job did you like the least and why?

Interview Sheet, continued

8. Are you aware of the many duties that are required of a licensed assistant?

9. How do you feel about working some weekends?

10. Would you be willing to show property to some of my clients, and write offers for me if it were necessary and a bonus were included?

11. If you are selected, you will need to supply me with the names of at least two former clients and two agents as references. Will you do that?

12. If an angry client called and was verbally abusive to you, how would you handle it?

13. What questions do you have for me at this time?

Escrow Checklist
(Home Sale)

❏ Open escrow. Notify all parties of the escrow agent or closing attorney's information. Get purchase contract and deposit check to escrow or verify that the deposit is at escrow if it is your agent's listing. Provide all client and agent information to escrow.

❏ If this is a new subdivision sale, verify that the buyers have signed for and received a copy of the Final Subdivision Public Report from the developer, if needed.

❏ Send Disclosure Statement information to the buyer's agent or obtain it from the listing agent as necessary.

❏ Obtain a Comprehensive Loss Underwriting Exchange (CLUE) report from the appropriate party.

❏ Order any inspections required around the agent's schedule, or notify the agent of the inspection times and dates if it is his or her listing.

❏ Provide the buyer's lender with a copy of the purchase contract and title report.

❏ Obtain the Preliminary Title Report. Verify owners against the purchase contract. Review title exceptions for problematic issues and report findings to agent. Order a copy of easements and CC&Rs.

❏ Obtain and review Homeowner's Association documents. Notify the agent of any concerns.

❏ Order the required repairs, as directed by your agent, or verify with the listing agent that they have been performed.

Escrow Checklist
(Home Sale), continued

❏ See that the necessary property insurance has been ordered and sent to escrow or the closing attorney.

❏ Set up the walk-through reinspection date in conjunction with your agent's schedule.

❏ Update the agent and the client on a regular basis throughout the escrow.

❏ Meet the client for the agent at escrow signing, if requested.

❏ Prepare and submit all company and MLS Status Change forms.

❏ See that keys are obtained and/or delivered as necessary.

❏ Remove the MLS keybox, as necessary.

❏ Order the client-closing gift for the agent.

Escrow Checklist
(Income Property)

❏ Open escrow. Notify all parties of the escrow agent or closing attorney's information. Get purchase contract and deposit to escrow or verify that the deposit is at escrow if it is your agent's listing. Provide all client and agent information to escrow.

❏ Obtain copies of all leases currently in effect.

❏ Provide a copy of the purchase contract, title report, and leases to the buyer's lender and the buyer's agent, as appropriate.

❏ If a disclosure statement has been filled out by the seller, provide it to the buyer's agent or obtain it from the other agent. Give it to our client for review and signatures. Verify that it is returned to your file.

❏ Schedule a date to inspect the interior of the rental unit(s) and any other required inspections such as roof, termite, phase-1 environmental, etc., around your agent's schedule and notify him or her of the dates.

❏ Obtain a Comprehensive Loss Underwriting Exchange (CLUE) report from the appropriate party.

❏ Obtain the Preliminary Title report. Verify owners against the purchase contract. Review the title exceptions for problematic issues and report findings to agent. Order a copy of easements and CC&Rs.

❏ Prepare estoppel agreements or request title agency or closing attorney to do so. Obtain them from the listing agent if it is your agent's buyer.

Escrow Checklist
(Income Property), continued

❏ Update the agent and the client throughout the escrow.

❏ Set up reinspection date if repairs were required.

❏ Go to the closing on behalf of or with your agent, as requested.

❏ Prepare all company and/or MLS Status Change forms as necessary.

❏ See that keys are obtained and/or delivered as necessary.

❏ Order the client-closing gift for the agent.

Escrow Checklist
(Land)

❑ Open escrow. Notify all parties of the escrow agent or closing attorney's information. Get purchase contract and deposit check to escrow or verify that the deposit is at escrow if it is your agent's listing. Provide all client and agent information to escrow.

❑ Request and obtain copies of all CC&Rs and all other Homeowner Association documents as necessary.

❑ Obtain a copy of any required Land Affidavit and see that the appropriate parties receive it, sign it, and return it.

❑ If your agent's buyer is financing the purchase, provide the lender with a copy of the purchase contract and the title report.

❑ If it is your agent's buyer, ask the agent what inspections and/or reports are required and order them as necessary. Set the dates for inspections around your agent's time schedule. Such inspections may include, but are not limited to:

    ❑ Land survey.

    ❑ Percolation test.

    ❑ Staking and flagging the boundaries.

    ❑ Federal Emergency Management Agency (FEMA) flood map certification.

    ❑ Current zoning or viability of proposed zoning.

    ❑ Environmental reports such as a phase-1, phase-2, or phase-3 environmental report.

    ❑ Any proposed zoning or use changes proposed by a private or government agency in the immediate area that may affect the use or development of the land being sold.

Escrow Checklist
(Land), continued

☐ Obtain a report verifying that the property is not in a Federal Emergency Management Agency (FEMA) flood plain, if appropriate.

☐ Call the appropriate governing agency or go to the Internet and verify the current zoning. If you call a government agency, be sure to get the name of the person that you talked to.

☐ If there are any structures on the property, investigate their current occupancy status and report to your agent. If occupied, obtain a copy of any existing leases for review during the inspection period.

☐ If a seller's disclosure report exists, obtain a copy. Review it and give it to your agent with any notes. Deliver it to all appropriate parties for review and signatures.

☐ Verify that any flagging and/or staking of the boundaries was performed.

☐ Update the agent and the client throughout the escrow.

☐ Schedule the closing sign-off date.

☐ Go to the closing on behalf of or with your agent, as requested.

☐ Order the "For Sale" sign down if it is your listing.

☐ Order the client closing gift for the agent.

Appendix D

About the Author

Bob Herd started his real estate career in early 1972 with a small real estate company on the San Francisco Peninsula.

Although no formal training programs or systems were available in those days, Bob used some good initial training from his branch manager, his natural ability to interact with people, and his keen intuition about human nature to sell more than 60 homes his first and second years in the business. He was awarded the coveted "Top Salesperson" award from the real estate association that he belonged to in 1974.

Bob's wife, Eileen, was licensed in 1975 and became his licensed assistant on a part-time basis until their four children were grown; she then became his full-time assistant. Her help was very instrumental in his receipt of the "Top Salesperson" award and his continuing success throughout his career in sales.

Although Bob opened his own highly successful company in 1974, he still remained very active in sales, and under his training and guidance, one of his agents won the "Top Salesperson" award from the same association every year for the next six years, except for 1979.

Over the course of his career, which spans more than 32 years, Bob has been a salesperson, broker/owner, branch manager, and regional manager for some of the largest real estate companies in the San Francisco Bay area and Tucson, Arizona. Whether he was in a sales position or a non-selling management position, he always maintained and nurtured in his associates a keen sense of the ever-evolving sensible, human-nature-based style of professionally handling the needs of customers and clients and the far-reaching effectiveness of working with a top licensed assistant.

Bob maintains both a California and an Arizona broker's license and holds the Certified Residential Brokerage Manager (CRB), Certified Residential Specialist (CRS), and Graduate, Realtors Institute (GRI) designations. He is currently a branch manager for Coldwell Banker Success Southwest in Tucson, Arizona. You may reach Bob at (520) 240-2403 or by e-mail at rlherd@comcast.net.

Index

Index

Index

Index

Index

V

vacation, 1, 8, 64, 81, 98
vacation coverage, 63, 113, 127
verification, 58
    of acreage, 58
    of bank accounts, 4
    of school system, 58
    size of lot, 58
    square footage of structure, 58
voice mail, 62

W

Website, 75, 93, 94, 97, 98, 126, 101, 127, 131
    maintaining, 97
    updating, 97
    uploading pictures, 101

weekends, 64
    coverage, 63, 113, 127
Women's Council of
    REALTORS®, 33
work ethic, 35, 48
work schedule, 44, 46
workload, reasonable, 55
writing offers, 3
writing purchase contracts, 15
written contract, 80
Written Disclosure Statement, 58
wrongful termination suit, 40

Z

zoning, 58